Simply Sensational
SQUARE-AGONALS® QUILTS

by Sandi Blackwell

Landauer Publishing, LLC

Simply Sensational
SQUARE-AGONALS® QUILTS

by Sandi Blackwell

Copyright© 2013 by Landauer Publishing, LLC

Square-agonals®
Project Designs Copyright© 2012 by Sandi Blackwell

This book was designed, produced, and
published by Landauer Publishing, LLC
3100 101st Street, Urbandale, IA 50322
www.landauerpub.com   800/557-2144   515/287-2144

President/Publisher: Jeramy Lanigan Landauer
Vice President of Sales and Administration: Kitty Jacobson
Editor: Jeri Simon
Art Director: Laurel Albright
Photographer: Sue Voegtlin

ISBN 13: 978-1-935726-35-7
Library of Congress
Control Number: 2012956104

This book printed on acid-free paper.
Printed in United States

10-9-8-7-6-5-4-3-2-1

Introduction

Square-agonals® is a simple way to create quilts with a diagonal setting without adding setting and corner triangles. This method will make your quilt piecing easier and more creative.

Your quilt top is stitched together in rows of squares that are pieced, appliquéd, directional, or solid. The quilt top is then cut into three sections and reassembled in a new configuration. The result is a finished design in a diagonal setting. All sizes of blocks and quilt tops can utilize this technique. The secret is the layout of the blocks and where you make your cuts.

The quilt designs created for you in this book will take you to the next level of Square-agonals® and quilt making. Complex designs can be sewn with ease using this method. That is the beauty of Square-agonals®, you can create a quilt that looks complicated and detailed, yet have the tools to put it together with simple blocks and steps. I hope you enjoy these new designs.

Read the Square-agonals® instructions and tips before starting a project. Carefully follow the layout and sewing instructions for each pattern.

Words to Sew by:

Patience, creativity, and a sense of humor will go a long way in your quiltmaking enjoyment.

Let yourself enjoy the process and the journey. Be willing to learn from your mistakes.

Keep your quilting fun and stress free. There are no quilt police, your quilt is your own creation.

Admire your work, imperfections and all.

Table of Contents

The Mathematics of Square-agonals®

Quilting: science becoming art

Note: this information is for your inquisitive mind only.
You do not need to know or understand it in order to sew the quilts.

Quilting is enjoyable on many levels. Perhaps it is because it challenges the artistic side of the brain as well as the logical side. Square-agonals® is a great example of this challenge since it is based upon an area of mathematics often referred to as 'dissection'.

There are many artistic and fun dissections you can find on the internet, but the specific example that Square-agonals® uses is one with a lucky coincidence. This dissection has the fortunate result of putting the inside cut edges outside, and rotating the previous rectangle 45-degrees thus creating side and corner triangles.

To turn a rectangle into a square, or a square into a rectangle, the following geometric formula is used.

A rectangle with sides A and B.
Side A must be smaller than side B.
Side B can be no larger than twice the length of side A.
  (Note: For this equation to work on a Square-agonals® quilt, the lengths of side A and side B must be carefully considered.)

Calculate $S = \sqrt{A*B}$ and draw a line from one of the corners across diagonally to the other side. Draw the second line, perpendicular to the S line from the other corner.

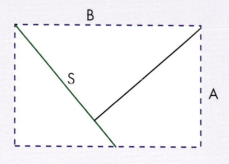

Cut the rectangle into the three pieces and reassemble.

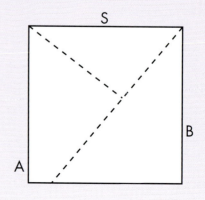

Square-agonals® Instructions

Preparing your fabric

1 Following your selected pattern, carefully lay out all your quilt blocks according to the Sewing & Cutting Diagram in the pattern. You must keep the blocks in the correct position to achieve the finished layout. Sew the blocks together in rows, and then sew the rows together. To assist you in keeping the rows in the correct position, mark the first block in each row with a piece of paper indicating the row number and stack the blocks together in each row.

2 Press the seam allowances in opposite directions for each row so the blocks will lay flat when you sew the rows together. Once the blocks are sewn together, press the quilt top with starch. Be sure to heavily starch the blocks that will be cut. This step is very important in order to keep the bias edges from stretching while being handled.

Sew

3 Refer to the Sewing & Cutting Diagram for the cutting lines and mark them carefully using a ruler and pencil. The lines will end up in the seam allowance and won't show on the finished quilt.

Optional: Use the Square-agonals® Cutting Guide Tape shown on page 9.

4 Mark each section with an arrow template as shown in each pattern. This will help you reassemble the top with ease. When the pieces are reassembled, all the arrows should point to the bottom. Arrow templates are on page 12.

Optional: Use the Square-agonals® Arrow Guide Tape shown on page 9.

5 Double check the pattern to make sure you are cutting on the correct lines. Cut on the pencil lines using your rotary cutter, acrylic ruler, and mat. You need to cut the line marked "cut first" first. It is easier if you move the mat underneath the quilt top and cut in small sections from one end to the other. You will be cutting from a block corner point to the next block corner point across the quilt top. Take your time. Correct cutting is the most important step.

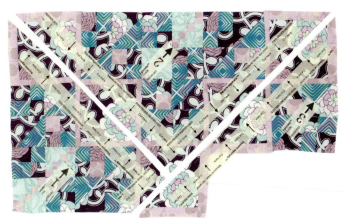

Cut

6 Once the quilt top is cut avoid any excess handling, since you have now exposed the bias edges. Lay out the three sections as shown in the Reassemble Diagram. Pin the sections together at each seam allowance.

You may need to flip some of the seam allowances in opposite directions to nest the seams together.

Reassemble

7 Take your time and sew the sections together. You will now have one or two corners that will need trimmed from an overhanging block. Use a square up ruler to trim them.

Diagonal Setting

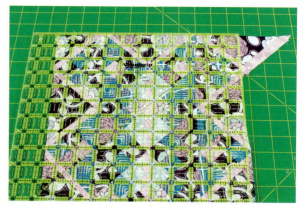

8 The top is now ready to add borders. You need to handle the top carefully due to the exposed bias edges.

Adding Borders:

NOTE: The project instructions have been written with the border strips cut on the crosswise grain and then pieced together. If you do not wish to piece your border, cut your border strips on the lengthwise grain. You will need to purchase extra fabric if cutting on the lengthwise grain.

Side Borders

1 Measure the length of the quilt top through the center from top to bottom. Use this measurement to trim the cut length of the prepared border strips. You will add these borders to the sides of your quilt.

2 Find the midpoint of your borders and quilt top by folding each one in half. Press a fold line on the center marks. Match the center mark of the borders to the center mark of the quilt top and pin in place.

3 Line up the ends of your borders to the ends of your quilt and pin in place. Insert additional pins, easing in fabric as needed. Always sew with the border strips on top so you can ease in any of the quilt top's bias stretch. Sew slowly to go over the extra bulk you have in the seam allowances. Sew the borders to the sides of the quilt center. Press the seam allowances away from the quilt center.

Top and Bottom Borders

1 Measure the width of your quilt top through the center from side to side. Use this measurement to cut the prepared border strips to length. You will add these borders to the top and bottom of your quilt.

2 Find the midpoint of your borders and quilt top by folding in half. Press a fold line on the center marks. Match the center mark of the borders to the center mark of the quilt top and pin in place. Line up the ends of your borders to the ends of your quilt and pin in place. Insert additional pins, easing in fabric as needed. Sew the borders to the top and bottom edges of the quilt center. Press the seam allowances away from the quilt center.

NOTE: When you add your sashings and first borders you will nip off the tips of the diagonal set triangles, this is part of the design and a distinguishing feature of Square-agonals® quilts called the Square-agonals® Signature!

3 Repeat this process for any additional border strips.

Optional Guide Tapes
"I'm afraid to cut my quilt!"

Trust me I understand. To add to your confidence and make the entire process easier to handle and understand, I have developed two lines of guide tape. The guide tape, along with the directions and illustrations in the book, will have you cutting and reassembling your quilt blocks into a beautiful diagonal design with complete confidence. Although many quilters find these products a wonderful aid in making their Square-agonals® quilts, they are not required to complete any of the projects in this book.

Cutting Guide Tape: I designed this tape to give you a "comfort" zone when cutting your quilt top. Line up the tape's arrows 1/4" away from the cutting lines. Use it with your drawn line. The tape will give a clearer visual guide of where the cuts are to be made. If you place the tape on both sides of the cutting lines, all sections with tape will be on the outside edges of the quilt after you cut the top. This will serve as another guide when reassembling the pieces and add extra stability for the exposed bias edges. Keep your tape in place until you are ready to add the borders.

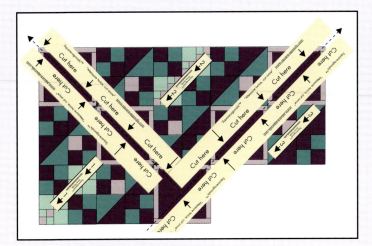

Arrow Guide Tape: Use this tape in place of the paper arrows from the book. The arrows can be placed on the quilt sections and easily re-aligned if necessary. Follow the illustrations in each project for the correct placement of the arrows. The arrows make reassembly easier.

Square-agonals® Sewing Tips

Fabric Cutting:

- Cut all borders first. My measurements include an extra inch or two so you will need to trim the borders to the finished size.

- Cut your block pieces accurately.

- Mark all pieces that have a template letter.

Sewing:

- Sew with a consistent 1/4" seam allowance.

- Mark seam allowances when necessary.

- To easily control rows of blocks, use slips of paper and mark the first block in row one with a #1, row two with a #2, etc. Stack all the blocks in the correct order for each row behind each marked block.

- Always sew the borders with the border on the top so the feed dogs can ease in any stretched fabric.

Square-agonals® Cutting:

- Double check your sewing layout before marking and cutting.

- Heavily starch (do not use sizing) the quilt top, especially the cutting line blocks.

- Lightly draw your cutting line. Optional; use the Square-agonals® Cutting Guide Tape.

- Mark your sections with arrows marked 1, 2, and 3. Arrow templates are provided on page 12 for you to copy and use. Optional; use the Square-agonals® Arrow Guide Tape.

- Position the arrows in the directions shown in the Sewing & Cutting Diagram. This will help you reassemble the top with ease. When the pieces are reassembled, all the arrows should point in one direction.

- You will cut on the line marked "cut first", usually the longest line, then cut the remaining line.

- You will be cutting from a block corner point to the next block corner point across the quilt top.

- When you cut from a corner block the cut will start in the point.

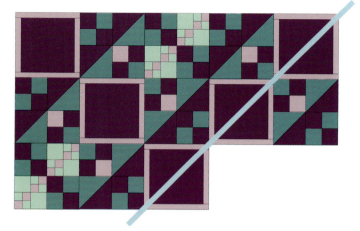

- When your cut ends in a block that is not on the end you will be cutting 1/4 into the next block.

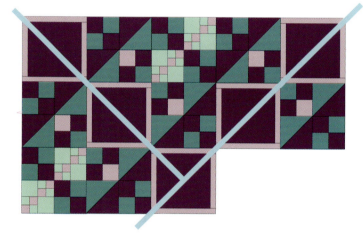

- Do not trim away any excess fabric until the top is sewn back together.

Square-agonals® Sewing:

- You will sew two sections together first, then add the last section.

- Carefully sew the sections together, matching seam allowances, and handling edges carefully.

- If you use the Cutting Guide Tape, do not remove until ready to add borders. It will add extra stability to the bias edges during handling.

- You may need to flip seam allowances to opposite directions to nest the seams together.

- Use a square up ruler to carefully trim any excess overhanging fabric in the corners.

Basic Needs

Iron: A hot iron is needed to press your fabric pieces as you sew them together. It is also essential for the final pressing before you cut the quilt top into three pieces. To avoid excess stretching, do not use steam on bias edges.

Starch: Starch is absolutely necessary to prevent overstretching of exposed bias edges. When you cut your quilt top on the designated blocks you will be exposing the bias edges. The starch will give the fabric stiffness, help eliminate any stretching, and make the final piecing easier.

Sewing Machine: Working with a well maintained sewing machine is a joy. Make sure your machine is clean and in good working order. Make a habit of replacing your needle before every new project.

Straight Pins: The small cost of quality quilting straight pins is well worth the price. A lot of pinning is required in this technique to ensure accuracy in your piecing.

Square-agonals® Guide Tapes: The Cutting Guide Tape and Arrow Guide Tape are optional but will make the Square-agonals® process easier. Ask for them at your local quilt shop. You may also purchase directly from www.stitchedbuy.com.

Rotary Cutter: A rotary cutter is an essential part of quilting today. I recommend you start each new project with a new blade.

Rulers and Cutting Mats: An 18" or 24" acrylic ruler and an 18" x 24", or larger, cutting mat will make cutting your quilt top easy. You will be able to slide the mat under the quilt and the size of the ruler will make it easier to move along the fabric to cut the length you need. These sizes also help cut fabric selvage to selvage because you can cut the strips with only one fold of the fabric. The more folds of the fabric you have, the more likely you are to get "bends" in your strips. A square-up ruler is also helpful in trimming the overhanging block sections and checking block sizes.

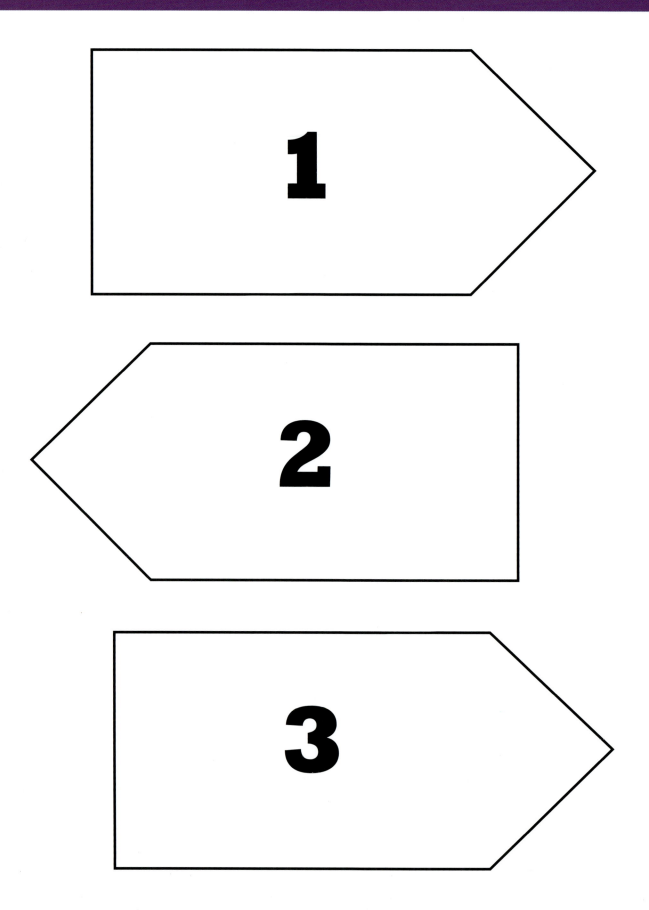

The Projects

STONES IN THE STREAM

Pieced by Doris Turk

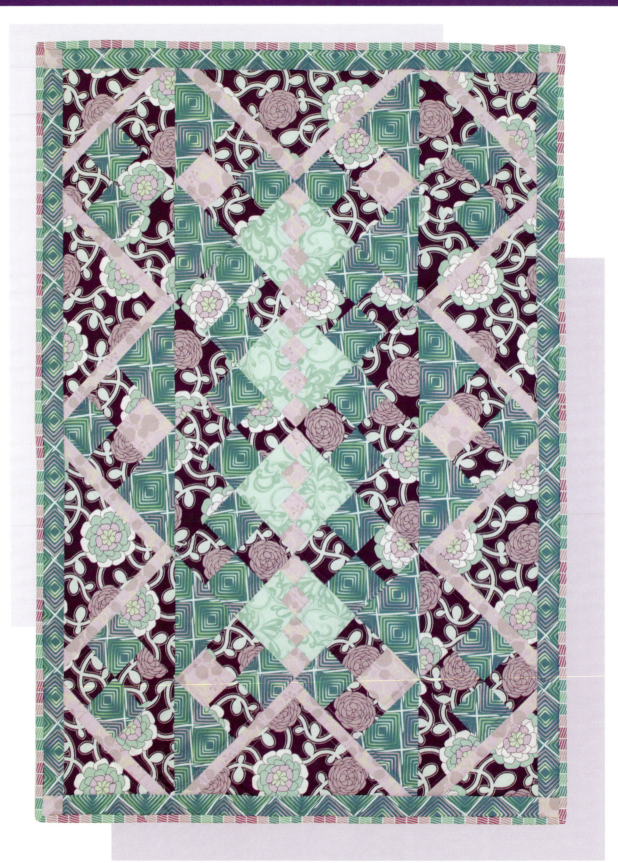

Finished Size:
25" x 36"

Block Size:
8" square

Materials
3/4 yard dark purple fabric for blocks

3/4 yard dark teal fabric for blocks and border

1/2 yard light purple fabric for blocks and border corners

1/4 yard light teal fabric for blocks

1/3 yard stripe fabric for binding

1-1/2 yards backing fabric

31" x 42" piece of batting

Refer to Square-agonals® Instructions and Sewing Tips on pages 7-10.

To make a 13" x 19" version of the Stones in the Stream quilt, refer to page 18 for Materials and Cutting Instructions.

Doris Block	Pebbles Block	Linda Block
		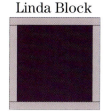

Cutting Instructions

From dark purple fabric, cut:
(1) 7-1/8" x 40" strip.
  From the strip, cut: (5) 7-1/8" C squares for Linda Block.
(1) 4-7/8" x 40" strip.
  From the strip, cut: (6) 4-7/8" squares. Cut the squares in half diagonally to make 12 A triangles for Doris Block.
(2) 2-1/2" x 40" strips.
  From the strips, cut: (32) 2-1/2" B squares for Doris Block and A squares for Pebbles Block.

From dark teal fabric, cut:
(2) 4-7/8" x 40" strip.
  From the strips, cut: (6) 4-7/8" squares. Cut the squares in half diagonally to make 12 A triangles for Doris Block
(2) 2-1/2" x 40" strip.
  From the strip, cut: (26) 2-1/2" B squares for Doris Block and A squares for Pebbles Block.
(4) 1-1/2" x 40" strips for border.

From light purple fabric, cut:
(1) 2-1/2" x 40" strip.
  From the strip, cut: (6) 2-1/2" B squares for Doris Block.
(1) 1-1/2" x 40" strip.
  From the strip, cut: (20) 1-1/2" B squares for Pebbles Block and border corners.
(3) 1-1/8" x 40" strips.
  From the strips, cut: (10) 1-1/8" x 8-1/2" A rectangles for Linda Block.
(2) 1-1/8" x 40" strips.
  From the strips, cut: (10) 1-1/8" x 7-1/8" B rectangles for Linda Block.

From light teal fabric, cut:
(1) 2-1/2" x 40" strip.
  From the strip, cut: (8) 2-1/2" A squares for Pebbles Block.
(1) 1-1/2" x 40" strip.
  From the strip, cut: (16) 1-1/2" B squares for Pebbles Block.

From stripe fabric, cut:
(4) 2-1/2" x 40" binding strips.

From backing fabric, cut:
(1) 31" x 42" rectangle.

15

Making the Doris Block

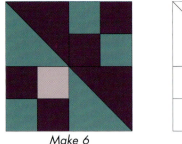
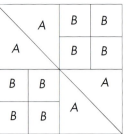

Make 6

1. Lay out 2 dark purple A triangles, 2 dark teal A triangles, 4 dark purple B squares, 3 dark teal B squares, and one light purple B square, as shown.

2. Sew along the long edge of a dark purple A triangle and dark teal A triangle, right sides together, to make a half-square triangle. Make 2 dark purple/dark teal half-square triangles.

3. Sew a dark purple B square and a dark teal B square together. Repeat to make 2 pairs. Join the pairs together to make 1 four-patch unit.

4. Sew a dark purple B square and a light purple B square together. Sew a dark teal B square and a dark purple B square together. Sew the pairs together to make 1 four-patch unit.

5. Arrange the 2 half-square triangles with the 2 four-patch units as shown in the Doris Block. Sew the pieces together in rows. Sew the rows together.

6. Repeat steps 1-5 to make a total of 6 Doris Blocks.

Making the Pebbles Block

1. Lay out 4 dark purple A squares, 4 dark teal A squares, 4 light teal A squares, 8 light teal B squares, and 8 light purple B squares, as shown.

Make 2

2. Sew a dark purple A square and a dark teal A square together. Repeat to make 2 pairs. Join the pairs together to make 1 dark purple/dark teal four-patch unit. Make a total of 2 dark purple/dark teal four-patch units.

3. Sew a light purple B square and a light teal B square together. Repeat to make 2 pairs. Join the pairs to make 1 light purple/light teal four-patch unit. Make a total of 4 light purple/light teal four-patch units.

4. Sew a light teal A square and a light purple/light teal four-patch unit together in pairs. Make a total of 4 pairs. Join 2 pairs together to make a large four-patch block. Make a total of 2 large four-patch units.

5. Lay out 2 dark purple/dark teal four-patch units and 2 large four-patch units as shown in the Pebbles Block. Sew the blocks together in rows. Sew the rows together. Make a total of 2 Pebbles Blocks.

Making the Linda Block

1. Lay out a dark purple C square, 2 light purple A rectangles, and 2 light purple B rectangles, as shown.

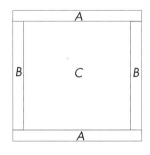

Make 5

2. Sew the light purple B rectangles to opposite sides of the dark purple C square. Press away from the center.

3. Sew the light purple A rectangles to the remaining sides of the dark purple square C.

4. Repeat steps 1-3 to make a total of 5 Linda Blocks.

Assembling the Quilt Center

1. Lay out the 6 Doris Blocks, 2 Pebbles Blocks, and 5 Linda Blocks on a flat surface as shown in the *Sewing & Cutting Diagram*. Take care to place the blocks in the correct position to achieve the final quilt design.

2. Sew the blocks together into rows. Press the seams of each row to one side, alternating the direction with each row. Sew the rows together, adding the partial row on the bottom, as shown.

3. Press your quilt top with starch to prepare it for cutting. Referring to the *Sewing & Cutting Diagram*, use a pencil and ruler to mark the cutting lines and label the sections with arrows in the directions shown. Carefully cut the top into 3 sections on the pencil lines.

Note: Refer to page 9 if using the Cutting Guide and Arrow Guide Tape.

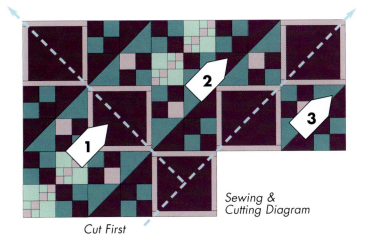

Cut First

Sewing & Cutting Diagram

4. Lay out the sections as shown in the *Reassemble Diagram* with the arrows pointing down. Sew the sections together and press. Trim the excess fabric in the corners with a square up ruler to complete the quilt center.

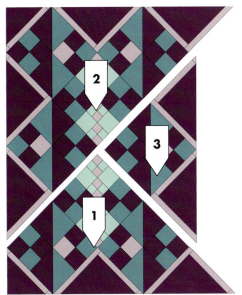

Reassemble Diagram

Adding the Borders

1. Measure your quilt center and cut the four dark teal border strip sections to size. Sew the side borders to the left and right edges of the quilt center. Press seams toward the borders.

2. Sew a light purple 1-1/2" square to each end of the top and bottom border strips. Sew these borders to the top and bottom edges of the quilt center. Press seams toward the borders.

Finishing the Quilt

1. Layer the backing, batting, and the quilt top. Baste the layers together and hand- or machine quilt as desired.

2. Use diagonal seams to sew the 2-1/2" wide stripe binding strips together to make one long strip. Sew the binding to the edges of the quilt top.

3. Trim the extra batting and backing even with the edges of the quilt top. Turn the binding over the edge to the back and hand- or machine sew in place.

Stones in the Stream Quilt

Finished Size: 13" x 19"

Block Size: 4" square

1/3 yard dark purple for blocks

1/4 yard dark teal for blocks and border

1/4 yard light purple for blocks and border corners

1/8 yard light teal for blocks

1/4 yard stripe fabric for binding

7/8 yard backing fabric

19" x 25" piece of batting

From dark purple fabric, cut:
- (1) 3-7/8" x 40" strip.
  From the strip, cut: (5) 3-7/8" C squares for Linda Block.
- (1) 2-7/8" x 40" strip.
  From the strip, cut: (6) 2-7/8" squares. Cut the squares in half diagonally to make 12 A triangles for Doris Block.
- (2) 1-1/2" x 40" strips.
  From the strips, cut: (32) 1-1/2" B squares for Doris Block and A squares for Pebbles Block.

From dark teal fabric, cut:
- (1) 2-7/8" x 40" strip.
  From the strip, cut: (6) 2-7/8" squares. Cut the squares in half diagonally to make 12 A triangles for Doris Block
- (1) 1-1/2" x 40" strip.
  From the strip, cut: (26) 1-1/2" B squares for Doris Block and A squares for Pebbles Block.
- (2) 1-1/2" x 40" strips for border.

From light purple fabric, cut:
- (1) 1-1/2" x 40" strip.
  From the strip, cut: (6) 1-1/2" B squares for Doris Block.
- (1) 1" x 40" strip.
  From the strip, cut: (20) 1" B squares for Pebbles Block and border corners.

- (2) 7/8" x 40" strips.
  From the strips, cut: (10) 7/8" x 4-1/2" A rectangles for Linda Block.
- (1) 7/8" x 40" strips.
  From the strip, cut: (10) 7/8" x 3-7/8" B rectangles for Linda Block.

From light teal fabric, cut:
- (1) 1-1/2" x 40" strip.
  From the strip, cut: (8) 1-1/2" A squares for Pebbles Block.
- (1) 1" x 40" strip.
  From the strip, cut: (16) 1" B squares for Pebbles Block.

From stripe fabric, cut:
- (2) 2-1/2" x 40" binding strips.

From backing fabric, cut:
- (1) 19" x 25" rectangle.

Stones in the Stream

GREEN TEA

Pieced by Susan Collins

Finished Size:
21" x 46"

Block Size:
6" square

Materials

1 yard green fabric for blocks and binding

3/4 yard pink fabric for blocks and borders

3/4 yard floral fabric for blocks

1-1/2 yards backing fabric

27" x 52" piece of batting

Refer to Square-agonals® Instructions and Sewing Tips on pages 7-10.

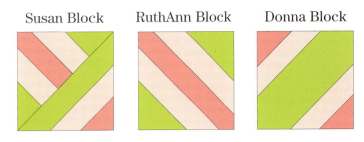

Susan Block   RuthAnn Block   Donna Block

Cutting Instructions

From green fabric, cut:
(1) 4-1/4" x 40" strip.
   From the strip, cut: (8) 4-1/4" squares. Cut the squares into quarters diagonally to make 32 C triangles for Susan Block.
(1) 3-7/8" x 40" strip.
   From the strip, cut: (4) 3-7/8" squares. Cut the squares in half diagonally to make 8 C triangles for RuthAnn Block.
(2) template C on page 27 for Donna Block.
(4) 2-1/2" x 40" binding strips.
(4) 2" x 40" strips.
   From the strips, cut: 15 template D on page 25 for Susan Block.

From pink fabric, cut:
(1) 2-7/8" x 40" strip.
   From the strip, cut: (10) 2-7/8" squares. Cut the squares in half diagonally to make a total of 20 triangles for F in Susan Block and A in Donna Block.
(4) 2-1/2" x 40" strips for borders.
(3) 1-7/8" x 40" strips.
   From the strips, cut: (4) template A on page 26 for RuthAnn Block and (15) template A on page 24 for Susan Block.

From floral fabric, cut:
(6) 2" x 40" strips.
   From the strips, cut: (15) template B on page 24 and (15) template G on page 24 for Susan Block.
   Also, cut (8) template B on page 26 for RuthAnn Block.
(4) 1-7/8" x 40" strips.
   From the strips, cut: (15) template E on page 25 for Susan Block and (4) template B on page 27 for Donna Block.

From backing fabric, cut:
(1) 27" x 52" rectangle.

Making the Susan Block

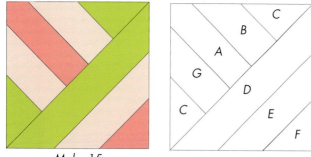

Make 15

1. Lay out 2 green C triangles, 1 green D piece, 1 pink F triangle, 1 pink A piece, 1 floral B piece, 1 floral G piece, and 1 floral E piece. Mark all seam allowances for easy piecing.

2. Sew the green D piece to the floral E piece, matching seam allowances. Sew the pink F triangle to the opposite side of the floral E piece to make half of the Susan Block.

3. Sew the floral B and G pieces to opposite sides of the pink A piece, matching seam allowances.

4. Sew 2 green C triangles to opposite sides of the pink/floral unit from step 3 to make half of the Susan Block.

5. Sew the 2 halves of the Susan Block together to complete the block.

6. Repeat steps 1-5 to make a total of 15 Susan Blocks.

Making the RuthAnn Block

1. Lay out 2 green C triangles, 1 pink A piece, and 2 floral B pieces. Mark all seam allowances for easy piecing.

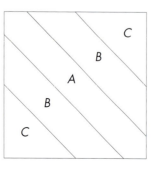

Make 4

2. Sew the floral B pieces to opposite sides of the pink A piece, matching seam allowances.

3. Sew the green C triangles to the floral B pieces to complete the block.

4. Repeat steps 1-3 to make a total of 4 RuthAnn Blocks.

Making the Donna Block

1. Lay out 2 pink A triangles, 1 green C piece, and 2 floral B pieces. Mark all seam allowances for easy piecing.

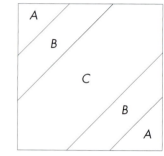

Make 2

2. Sew the floral B pieces to opposite sides of the green A piece, matching seam allowances.

3. Sew the pink A triangles to the floral B pieces to complete the block.

4. Repeat steps 1-3 to make a total of 2 Donna Blocks.

Assembling the Quilt Center

1. Lay out the 15 Susan Blocks, 4 RuthAnn Blocks, and 2 Donna Blocks on a flat surface as shown in the Sewing & Cutting Diagram. Take care to place the blocks in the correct position to achieve the final quilt design.

2. Sew the blocks together into rows. Press the seams of each row to one side, alternating the direction with each row. Sew the rows together, adding the single block on the top row.

3. Press your quilt top with starch to prepare it for cutting. Referring to the *Sewing & Cutting Diagram*, use a pencil and ruler to mark the cutting lines and label the sections with arrows in the directions shown. Carefully cut the top into 3 sections on the pencil lines.

Note: Refer to page 9 if using the Cutting Guide and Arrow Guide Tape.

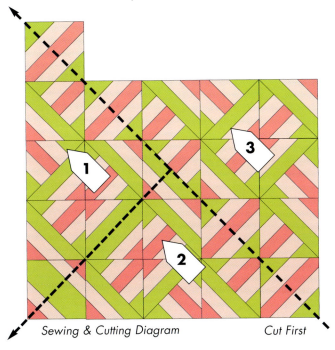

Sewing & Cutting Diagram   Cut First

4. Lay out the sections as shown in the *Reassemble Diagram* with the arrows pointing down. Sew the sections together and press. Trim the excess fabric in the corners with a square up ruler to complete the quilt center.

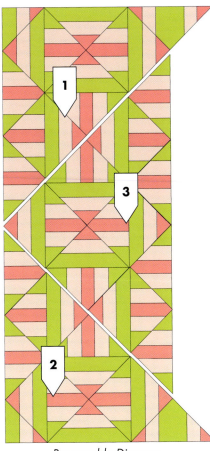

Reassemble Diagram

Adding the Borders

1. Sew together the 2-1/2"-wide pink border strips to make one long strip. Measure your quilt center from top to bottom and cut the two side border strips to size. Sew the borders to the side edges of the quilt center. Press seams toward the borders.

2. Measure the quilt center from side to side and cut the top and bottom border strips to size. Sew the borders to the top and bottom edges of the quilt center. Press seams toward the borders.

Finishing the Quilt

1. Layer the backing, the batting, and the quilt top. Baste the layers together and hand- or machine-quilt as desired.

2. Use diagonal seams to sew the 2-1/2"-wide green binding strips together to make one long strip. Sew the binding to the edges of the quilt top.

3. Trim the extra batting and backing even with the edges of the quilt top. Turn the binding over the edge to the back and hand- or machine-sew in place.

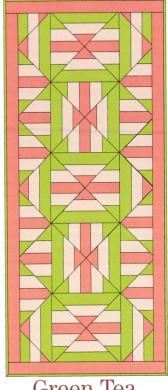

Green Tea

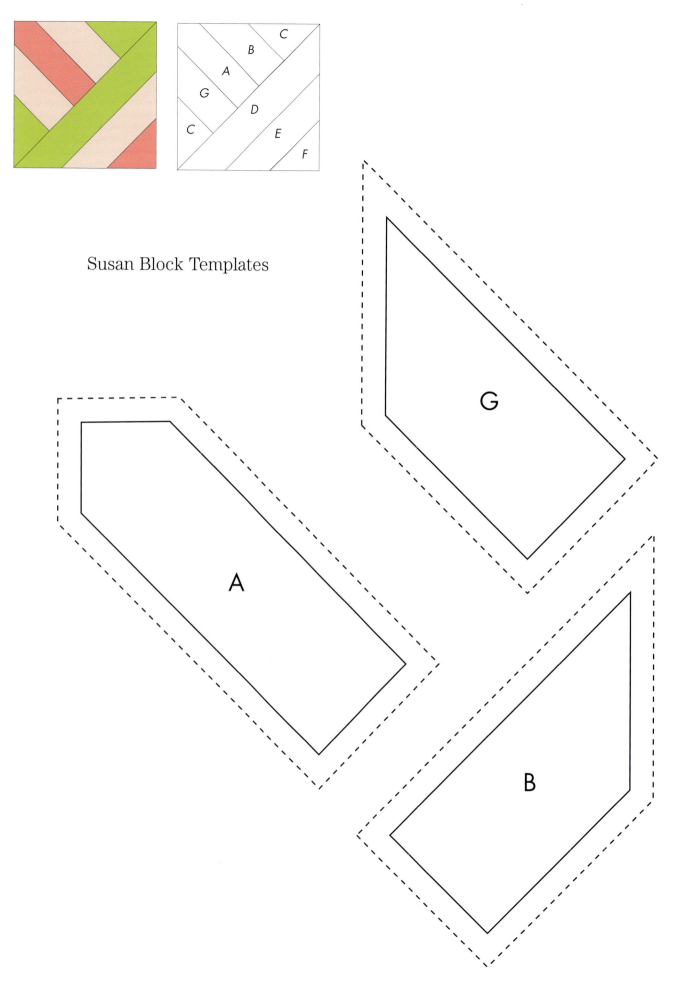

Susan Block Templates

Susan Block Templates

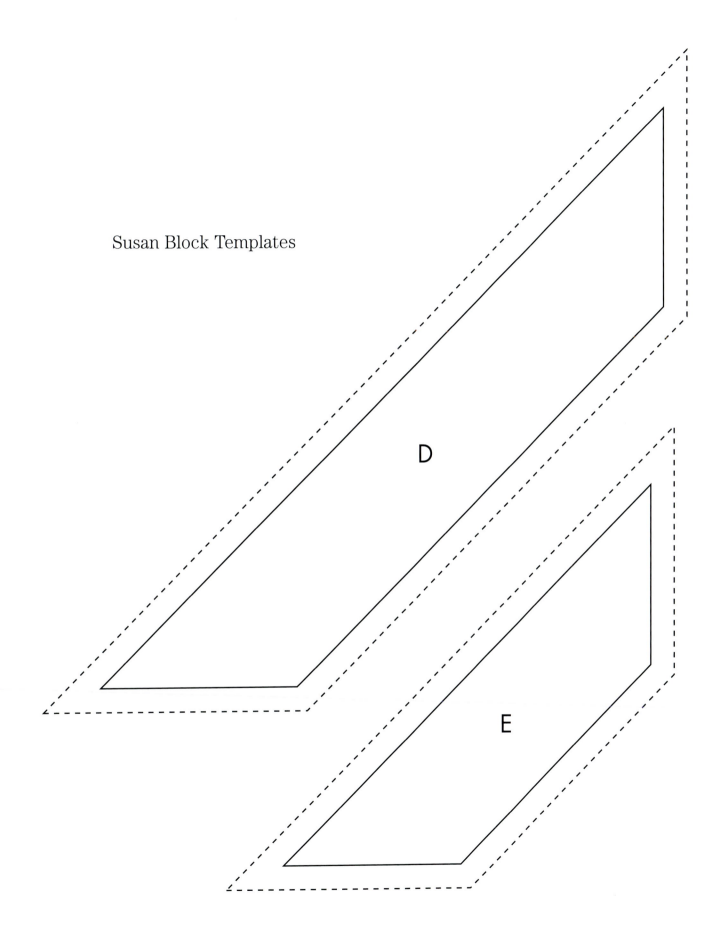

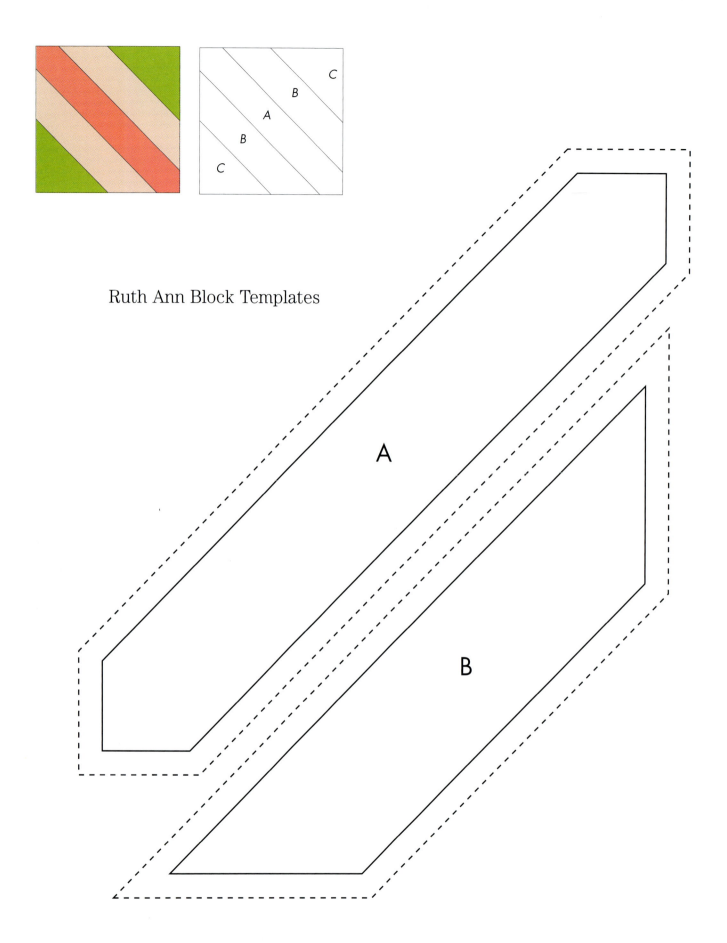

Ruth Ann Block Templates

A

B

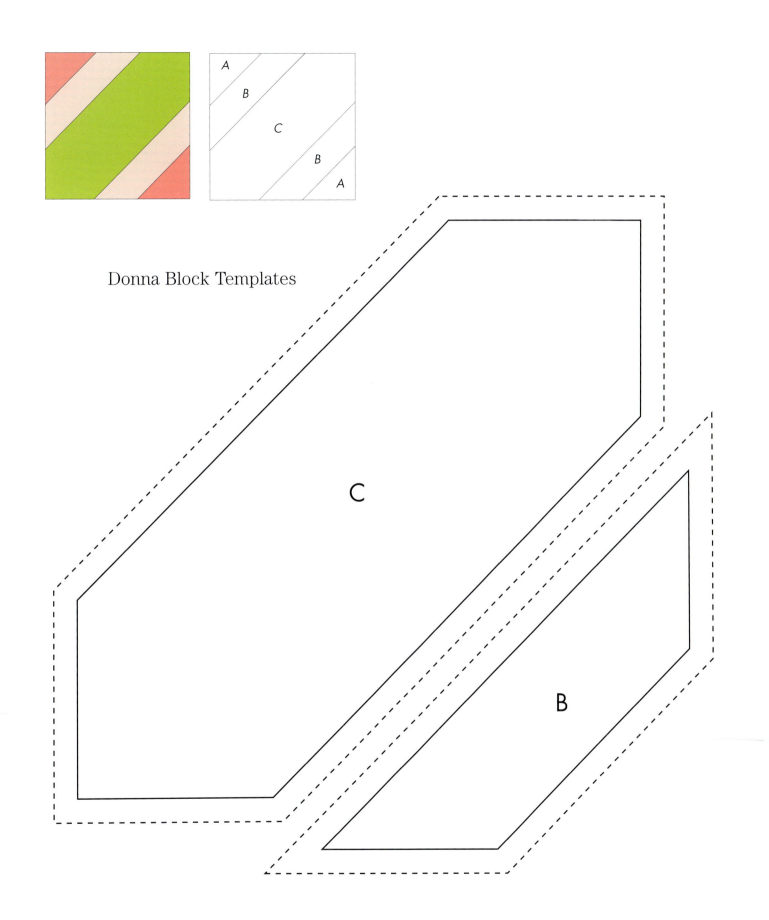

Donna Block Templates

C

B

VIOLET TRELLIS

Pieced by Judy Beveridge; quilted by Bev's Machine Quilting

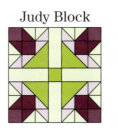
Judy Block

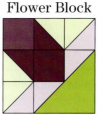
Flower Block

Finished Size:

20" x 48"

Block Size:

10" square

Materials:

7/8 yard dark purple fabric for blocks, borders, and binding

1/8 yard dark purple floral fabric for blocks

3/8 yard light purple fabric for blocks

1/2 yard green fabric for blocks and border

3/4 yard white print fabric for blocks and borders

1-5/8 yards backing fabric

26" x 54" piece batting

Refer to Square-agonals® Instructions and Sewing Tips on pages 7-10.

Cutting Instructions

From dark purple fabric, cut:
(4) 2-1/2" x 40" strips for binding.
(2) 2-1/4" x 40" strips.
   From the strips, cut: (28) 2-1/4" squares. Cut the squares in half diagonally to make 56 B triangles for Judy Block.
(2) 1-7/8" x 40" strips.
   From the strips, cut: (28) 1-7/8" A squares for Judy Block.
(3) 1-1/2" x 40" strips for borders.

From dark purple floral fabric, cut:
(2) 1-7/8" x 40" strips.
   From the strips, cut: (28) 1-7/8" A squares for Judy Block and (8) 1-1/2" squares for corner border nine-patch blocks.

From light purple fabric, cut:
(4) 2-1/4" x 40" strips.
   From the strips, cut: (56) 2-1/4" squares. Cut the squares in half diagonally to make 112 B triangles for Judy Block.

From green fabric, cut:
(2) 3-3/4" x 40" strips.
   From strips, cut: (14) 3-3/4" squares. Cut the squares in half diagonally to make 28 E triangles for Judy Block.
(1) 1-7/8" x 40" strip.
   From the strip, cut: (7) 1-7/8" A squares for Judy Block and (8) 1-1/2" squares for corner border nine-patch blocks.
(3) 1-1/2" x 40" strips for borders.

From white print fabric, cut:
(4) 2-1/4" x 40" strips.
   From the strips, cut: (56) 2-1/4" squares. Cut the squares in half diagonally to make 112 B triangles for Judy Block.
(4) 1-7/8" x 40" strips.
   From the strips, cut: (28) 1-7/8" x 4-3/4" C rectangles for Judy Block.
(3) 1-1/2" x 40" strips for borders.

(1) 1-1/2" x 40" strip.
   From the strip, cut: (20) 1-1/2" squares for corner border nine-patch blocks.

From backing fabric, cut:
(1) 26" x 54" rectangle.

Making the Judy Block

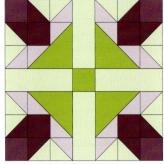 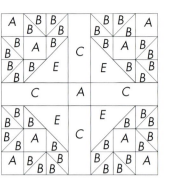

Make 7

1. Lay out the 8 dark purple B triangles, 16 light purple B triangles, 16 white print B triangles, 4 dark purple A squares, 4 dark purple floral A squares, 4 green E triangles, 1 green A square, and 4 white print C rectangles as shown.

2. Sew a light purple B triangle and a white print B triangle, right sides together, along the long edge to make a half-square triangle. Make a total 8 light purple/white print half-square triangles.

3. Sew a dark purple B triangle and a white print B triangle, right sides together, along the long edge to make a half-square triangle. Make a total 8 dark purple/white print half-square triangles.

4. Sew a dark purple A square and 2 light purple B triangles together as shown to make a triangle unit. Sew a green triangle E to the triangle unit to complete the square unit. Make a total of 4 dark purple/white print/green square units.

5. Sew 2 dark purple/white print half square triangles, 2 light purple/white print half square triangles, 1 dark purple flower A square, and the square unit together as shown to make a flower block. Make a total of 4 flower blocks.

6. Following the block layout, sew a flower block to opposite sides of a white print C rectangle to make a half block unit. Make a total of 2 half block units.

7. Sew a white print C rectangle to opposite sides of a green square A to make a sashing unit. Sew the half block units made in step 6 to opposite sides of the sashing unit to complete the Judy Block. Watch the direction of the flower blocks.

8. Repeat steps 1-7 to make a total of 7 Judy Blocks.

Assembling the Quilt Center

1. Lay out the 7 Judy Blocks on a flat surface as shown in the *Sewing & Cutting Diagram*. Take care to place the blocks in the correct position to achieve the final quilt design.

2. Sew the blocks together into rows. Press the seams of each row to one side, alternating the direction with each row. Sew the rows together, adding the single block on the bottom row.

3. Press your quilt top with starch to prepare it for cutting. Referring to the *Sewing & Cutting Diagram*, use a pencil and ruler to mark the cutting lines and label the sections with arrows in the directions shown. Carefully cut the top into 3 sections on the pencil lines.

Note: Refer to page 9 if using the Cutting Guide and Arrow Guide Tape.

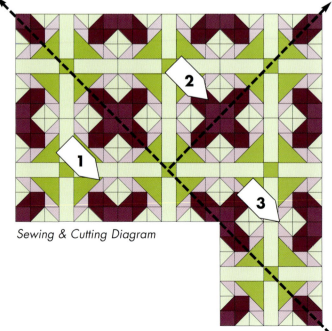

Sewing & Cutting Diagram

Cut First

4. Lay out the sections as shown in the *Reassemble Diagram* with the arrows pointing down. Sew the sections together and press. Trim the excess fabric in the corners with a square up ruler to complete the quilt center.

Reassemble Diagram

Making the Corner Border Nine-Patch Blocks

1. Lay out 2 dark purple floral squares, 2 green squares, and 5 white print squares to form the nine-patch border corners as shown.

2. Sew the blocks together in rows. Sew the rows together.

3. Repeat to make a total of 4 corner border nine-patch blocks.

Adding the Borders

1. Sew 3 dark purple 1-1/2" border strips together to make one long strip. Repeat with the 3 white print 1-1/2" border strips and the 3 green 1-1/2" border strips.

2. Sew the strips from step 1 together along the long edge and with the white print border strip in the center. Press seams away from the white strip. Handle these strips as one border strip.

3. Measure your quilt center and cut four border strip sections to size. Sew the borders to the left and right edges of the quilt center. Press seams toward the border.

4. Sew a corner border nine-patch block to each end of the top and bottom borders. Sew these borders to the top and bottom edges of the quilt center. Press seams toward the border.

Finishing the Quilt

1. Layer the backing, the batting, and the quilt top. Baste the layers together and hand- or machine-quilt as desired.

2. Use diagonal seams to sew the 2-1/2"-wide dark purple binding strips together to make one long strip. Sew the binding to the edges of the quilt top.

3. Trim the extra batting and backing even with the edges of the quilt top. Turn the binding over the edge to the back and hand- or machine-sew in place.

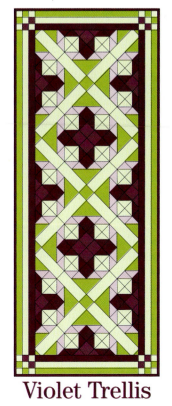

Violet Trellis

EASTER FLOWERS

Pieced by Ruth Ellen Fise; quilted by Bev's Machine Quilting

Finished Size:
45-1/2" x 45-1/2"

Block Size:
10" square

Materials

3/4 yard dark blue fabric for sashing, border, and binding

3/8 yard light blue fabric for sashing and border corners

1/4 yard dark green fabric for blocks and binding

5/8 yard light green fabric for blocks

1/4 yard dark yellow fabric for blocks and binding

5/8 yard light yellow fabric for blocks

1/4 yard dark orange fabric for blocks and binding

1/2 yard light orange for blocks

1/4 yard dark pink fabric for blocks and binding

5/8 yard light pink fabric for blocks

2-7/8 yards backing fabric

51" x 51" piece of batting

Refer to Square-agonals® Instructions and Sewing Tips on pages 7-10.

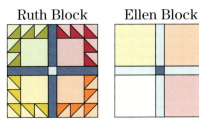

Ruth Block **Ellen Block**

Cutting Instructions

From dark blue fabric, cut:
(1) 2-1/2" x 40" strip for binding.
(5) 2" x 40" strips for borders.
(5) 1-1/2" x 40" strips.
   From the strips, cut: (36) 1-1/2" x 5"
   B rectangles for Ruth Block.
(1) 1-1/2" x 40" strip.
   From the strip, cut: (10) 1-1/2" C squares for Ellen Block.

From light blue fabric, cut:
(1) 2" x 40" strip.
   From the strip, cut: (4) 2" squares for border corners.
(6) 1-1/2" x 40" strips.
   From the strips, cut: (40) 1-1/2" x 5"
   B rectangles for Ellen Block and
   (9) 1-1/2" D squares for Ruth Block.

From dark green fabric, cut:
(1) 2-1/2" x 40" strip for binding.
(2) 2-3/8" x 40" strips.
   From the strips, cut: (23) 2-3/8" squares.
   Cut the squares in half diagonally to make
   46 A triangles for Ruth Block.

From light green fabric, cut:
(2) 5" x 40" strips.
   From the strips, cut: (10) 5" A squares for Ellen Block.
(1) 3-1/2" x 40" strip.
   From the strip, cut: (9) 3-1/2" C squares for Ruth Block.
(2) 2-3/8" x 40" strips.
   From the strips, cut: (23) 2-3/8" squares.
   Cut the squares in half diagonally to make
   46 A triangles for Ruth Block.

From dark yellow fabric, cut:
(1) 2-1/2" x 40" strip for binding.
(2) 2-3/8" x 40" strips.
   From the strips, cut: (23) 2-3/8" squares.
   Cut the squares in half diagonally to make
   46 A triangles for Ruth Block.

From light yellow fabric, cut:

- (2) 5" × 40" strips.
  From the strips, cut: (12) 5" A squares for Ellen Block.
- (1) 3-1/2" × 40" strip.
  From the strip, cut: (9) 3-1/2" C squares for Ruth Block.
- (2) 2-3/8" × 40" strips.
  From the strips, cut: (23) 2-3/8" squares. Cut the squares in half diagonally to make 46 A triangles for Ruth Block.

From dark orange fabric, cut:

- (1) 2-1/2" × 40" strip for binding.
- (2) 2-3/8" × 40" strips.
  From the strips, cut: (23) 2-3/8" squares. Cut the squares in half diagonally to make 46 A triangles for Ruth Block.

From light orange fabric, cut:

- (1) 5" × 40" strip.
  From the strip, cut: (6) 5" A squares for Ellen Block.
- (1) 3-1/2" × 40" strip.
  From the strip, cut: (9) 3-1/2" C squares for Ruth Block.
- (2) 2-3/8" × 40" strips.
  From the strips, cut: (23) 2-3/8" squares. Cut the squares in half diagonally to make 46 A triangles for Ruth Block.

From dark pink fabric, cut:

- (1) 2-1/2" × 40" strip for binding.
- (2) 2-3/8" × 40" strips.
  From the strips, cut: (23) 2-3/8" squares. Cut the squares in half diagonally to make 46 A triangles for Ruth Block.

From light pink fabric, cut:

- (2) 5" × 40" strips.
  From the strips, cut: (12) 5" A squares for Ellen Block.
- (1) 3-1/2" × 40" strip.
  From the strip, cut: (9) 3-1/2" C squares for Ruth Block.
- (2) 2-3/8" × 40" strips.
  From the strips, cut: (23) 2-3/8" squares. Cut the squares in half diagonally to make 46 A triangles for Ruth Block.

From backing fabric, cut:

- (2) 51" × 26" rectangles.

Making the Ruth Block

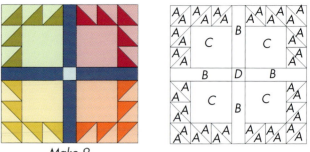

Make 9

1. Lay out 5 A triangles in each color—dark green, dark yellow, dark pink, dark orange, light green, light yellow, light pink, and light orange. Lay out 1 C square in each color—light green, light yellow, light pink, and light orange. As well as 4 dark blue D rectangles and 1 light blue D square as shown.

2. Sew a dark green A triangle and a light green A triangle, right sides together, along the long edge to make a half-square triangle. Make a total 5 dark green/light green half-square triangles.

3. Sew a dark yellow A triangle and a light yellow A triangle, right sides together, along the long edge to make a half-square triangle. Make a total 5 dark yellow/light yellow half-square triangles.

4. Sew a dark pink A triangle and a light pink A triangle, right sides together, along the long edge to make a half-square triangle. Make a total 5 dark pink/light pink half-square triangles.

5. Sew a dark orange A triangle and a light orange A triangle, right sides together, along the long edge to make a half-square triangle. Make a total 5 dark orange/light orange half-square triangles.

6. Sew 5 dark green/light green half square-triangles and 1 light green C square together as shown to make a corner block.

Repeat using the dark and light yellow, dark and light pink, and dark and light orange half-square triangles and C squares to make 1 corner block in each colorway.

7. Following the block layout, sew a green corner block and a yellow corner block on opposite sides of a dark blue B rectangle to make a half block unit.

8. Following the block layout, sew a pink corner block and an orange corner block on opposite sides of a dark blue B rectangle to make a half block unit.

9. Sew dark blue B rectangles to opposite sides of a light blue D square to make a sashing unit. Sew the two half block units to opposite sides of the sashing unit to complete the Ruth Block. Watch the direction of the half-square triangle blocks.

10. Repeat steps 1-9 to make a total of 9 Ruth Blocks.

Making the Ellen Block

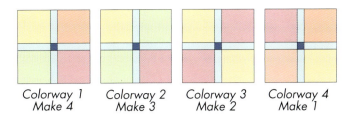

| Colorway 1 Make 4 | Colorway 2 Make 3 | Colorway 3 Make 2 | Colorway 4 Make 1 |

2. Following the block layout, sew a green A square and a yellow A square to opposite sides of a light blue B rectangle to make a half block unit.

3. Following the block layout, sew a pink A square and an orange A square to opposite sides of a light blue B rectangle to make a half block unit.

4. Sew light blue B rectangles to opposite sides of a dark blue C square to make a sashing unit. Sew the half block units to opposite sides of the sashing unit to complete the Ellen Block.

5. Repeat steps 1-4 to make a total of 4 Ellen Blocks in colorway 1.

6. Following steps 1-5 and using the color A squares as shown, sew the additional Ellen Blocks in the remaining 3 colorways.

Assembling the Quilt Center

1. Lay out the 9 Ruth Blocks and the 10 Ellen Blocks on a flat surface as shown in the *Sewing & Cutting Diagram*. Take care to place the blocks in the correct position to achieve the final quilt design.

2. Sew the blocks together into rows. Press the seams of each row to one side, alternating the direction with each row. Sew the rows together, adding the single block on the top row.

3. Press your quilt top with starch to prepare it for cutting. Referring to the *Sewing & Cutting Diagram*, use a pencil and ruler to mark the cutting lines and label the sections with arrows in the directions shown. Carefully cut the top into 3 sections on the pencil lines.

Make 10 in 4 colorways

A	B	A
B	C	B
A	B	A

1. Lay out 1 light green A square, 1 light yellow A square, 1 light pink A square, 1 light orange A square, 4 light blue B rectangles and 1 dark blue C square as shown.

Note: Refer to page 9 if using the Cutting Guide and Arrow Guide Tape.

4. Lay out the sections as shown in the *Reassemble Diagram* with the arrows pointing down. Sew the sections together and press. Trim the excess fabric in the corners with a square up ruler to complete the quilt center.

Adding the Borders

1. Sew the 2"-wide dark blue border strips together to make one long strip. Measure your quilt center and cut the 4 borders to size. Sew the borders to the left and right edges of the quilt center. Press seams toward the border.

2. Sew a light blue 2" square to each end of the top and bottom borders. Sew these borders to the top and bottom edges of the quilt center. Press seams toward the border.

Finishing the Quilt

1. Sew the 51" x 26" backing rectangles together along one long edge, using a 1/2" seam allowance. Press the seam allowance open.

2. Layer the backing, batting, and the quilt top. Baste the layers together and hand- or machine-quilt as desired.

3. Use diagonal seams to sew the five different color 2-1/2"- wide binding strips together to make one long strip. Sew the binding to the edges of the quilt top.

4. Trim the extra batting and backing even with the edges of the quilt top. Turn the binding over the edge to the back and hand- or machine-sew in place.

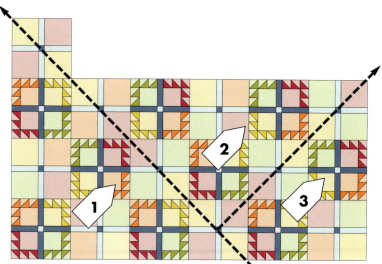

Sewing & Cutting Diagram   *Cut First*

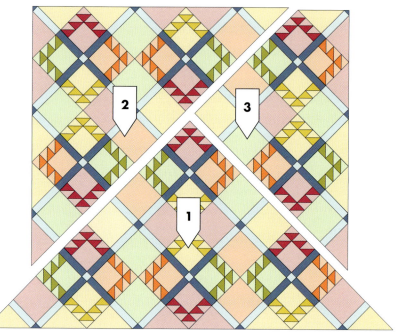

Reassemble Diagram

Easter Flowers

FOLLOW YOUR STAR

Pieced by Julia Plunkett; quilted by Finishing Touches Quilt Shop

Julia Block Friendship Star Blocks Nine-Patch Block

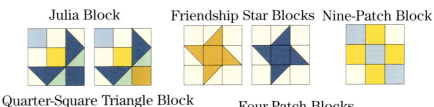

Quarter-Square Triangle Block

Four-Patch Blocks

Finished Size:
50" x 50"

Block Size:
4-1/2" square

Materials

7/8 yard dark teal fabric for blocks and borders

3/4 yard yellow floral fabric for blocks

1 yard dark yellow fabric for blocks, border corners and binding

3/4 yard medium yellow fabric for blocks

1 yard light yellow fabric for blocks

1/2 yard light teal fabric for blocks

3-1/4 yards backing fabric

56" x 56" piece of batting

Refer to Square-agonals® Instructions and Sewing Tips on pages 7-10.

To make a 99" x 99" version of the Follow Your Star quilt, refer to pages 43-44 for Materials and Cutting Instructions.

Cutting Instructions

From dark teal fabric, cut:
(1) 5-3/4" x 40" strip.
  From the strip, cut: (2) 5-3/4" squares.
  Cut the squares in quarters diagonally to make
  (8) A triangles for Quarter-Square Triangle Block.
(1) 4-1/4" x 40" strip.
  From the strip, cut: (8) 4-1/4" squares. Cut squares in quarters
  diagonally to make (32) C triangles for Julia Block.
(1) 2-3/4" x 40" strip.
  From the strip, cut: (2) 2-3/4" A squares for Four-Patch Block.
(1) 2-3/8" x 40" strip.
  From the strip, cut: (8) 2-3/8" squares. Cut squares in half
  diagonally to make (16) B triangles for Friendship Star Block.
(1) 2" x 40" strip.
  From the strip, cut: (12) 2" A squares for Julia Block and
  Friendship Star Block.
(6) 2" x 40" strips for outer border.

From dark yellow fabric, cut:
(1) 2-3/4" x 40" strip.
  From the strip, cut: (2) 2-3/4" A squares for Four-Patch Block.
(6) 2-1/2" x 40" strips for binding.
(1) 2-3/8" x 40" strip.
  From the strip, cut: (10) 2-3/8" squares. Cut squares in half
  diagonally to make (20) B triangles for Friendship Star Block.
(1) 2" x 40" strip.
  From the strip, cut: (13) 2" A squares for Friendship Star Block
  and Julia Block.
(5) 1-1/2" x 40" strips for inner border.

From yellow floral fabric, cut:
(1) 5-3/4" x 40" strip.
  From the strip, cut: (1) 5-3/4" square. Cut square in quarters
  diagonally to make (4) A triangles for Quarter-Square
  Triangle Block.
(3) 5" x 40" strips.
  From the strips, cut: (23) 5" squares.

(1) 2-3/8" x 40" strip.
  From the strip, cut: (16) 2-3/8" squares. Cut squares in half diagonally to make (32) B triangles for Julia Block.

From light teal fabric, cut:
(1) 5" x 40" strip.
  From the strip, cut: (7) 5" squares.
(1) 2-3/4" x 40" strip.
  From the strip, cut: (4) 2-3/4" A squares for Four-Patch Block
(4) 2" x 40" strips.
  From the strips, cut: (67) 2" A squares for Nine-Patch Block and Julia Block.

From medium yellow fabric, cut:
(2) 5" x 40" strips.
  From the strip, cut: (11) 5" squares.
(1) 2-3/4" x 40" strip.
  From the strip, cut: (4) 2-3/4" A squares for Four-Patch Block
(5) 2" x 40" strips.
  From the strips, cut: (84) 2" A squares for Nine-Patch Block and Julia Block.

From light yellow fabric, cut:
(1) 5-3/4" x 40" strip.
  From the strip, cut: (1) 5-3/4" square. Cut squares in quarters diagonally to make (4) A triangles for Quarter-Square Triangle Block.
(1) 5" x 40" strip.
  From the strip, cut: (7) 5" squares.
(1) 2-3/4" x 40" strip.
  From the strip, cut: (8) 2-3/4" A squares for Four-Patch Block.
(3) 2-3/8" x 40" strips.
  From the strips, cut: (34) 2-3/8" squares. Cut squares in half diagonally to make (68) B triangles for Julia Block and Friendship Star Block.
(6) 2" x 40" strips.
  From the strips, cut: (102) 2" A squares for Nine-Patch Block, Julia Block, and Friendship Star Block.

From backing fabric, cut:
(2) 56" x 29" rectangles.

Making the Julia Block

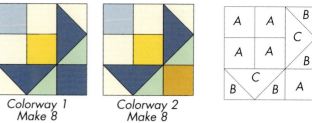

Colorway 1
Make 8

Colorway 2
Make 8

1. Lay out 2 dark teal C triangles, 2 yellow floral B triangles, 2 light yellow B triangles, 1 dark teal A square, 1 light teal A square, 2 light yellow A squares, and 1 medium yellow A square as shown in colorway 1.

2. Sew a light yellow B triangle to the left side of the dark teal C triangle and a yellow floral B triangle to the right side of the triangle to make a flying geese unit.

3. Make a second flying geese unit by sewing a light yellow B triangle to the right side of the dark teal C triangle and a yellow floral B triangle to the left side of the triangle.

4. Sew a light yellow A square to a light teal A square. Sew a light yellow A square to a medium yellow A square. Make a four-patch unit by sewing the two pairs together.

5. Referring to the Julia Block colorway 1, sew a flying geese unit with the yellow floral on the left side to the four-patch unit to make the top of the block.

6. Sew a dark teal A square to the end of the flying geese unit with the yellow floral on the right side to make the bottom of the block.

7. Sew the top and bottom units together to complete the Julia Block. Make a total of 8 Julia Blocks in colorway 1.

8. Repeat steps 1-7 to make 8 Julia Blocks in colorway 2. Replace the dark teal A square in step 6 with a dark yellow A square.

Making the Friendship Star Block

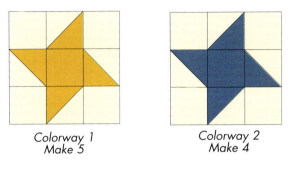

Colorway 1
Make 5

Colorway 2
Make 4

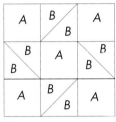

1. Lay out 4 light yellow A squares, 4 light yellow B triangles, 1 dark yellow A square, and 4 dark yellow B triangles, as shown in colorway 1.

2. Sew a light yellow B triangle and a dark yellow B triangle, right sides together, along the long edge to make a half-square triangle. Make a total of 4 half-square triangles.

3. Lay out 4 light yellow A squares, 1 dark yellow A square, and the 4 half-square triangles from step 2 to form the Friendship Star Block.

4. Sew the pieces together in rows. Press the seams of each row to one side, alternating the direction with each row. Sew the rows together.

5. Repeat steps 1-4 to make a total of 5 Friendship Star Blocks in colorway 1.

6. Follow steps 1-4 to make 4 Friendship Star Blocks in colorway 2. Replace the dark yellow A squares and B triangles in step 1 with the dark teal A squares and B triangles.

Making the Quarter-Square Triangle Block

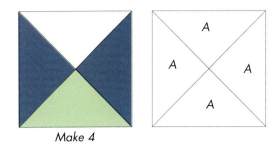

Make 4

1. Lay out 2 dark teal A triangles, 1 yellow floral A triangle, and 1 light yellow A triangle as shown.

2. Sew a light yellow triangle to a dark teal triangle to make half the block. Sew a yellow floral triangle to the remaining dark teal triangle to make the other half of the block.

3. Sew the two halves together to complete the block.

4. Repeat steps 1-3 to make a total of 4 Quarter-Square Triangle Blocks.

Making the Nine-Patch Block

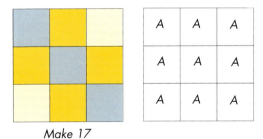

Make 17

1. Lay out 3 light teal A squares, 4 medium yellow A squares, and 2 light yellow A squares as shown.

2. Sew the squares into rows. Press the seams of each row to one side, alternating the direction with each row. Sew the rows together.

3. Repeat steps 1-2 to make a total of 17 Nine-Patch Blocks.

Making the Four-Patch Block

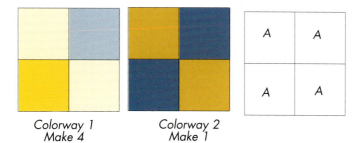

Colorway 1
Make 4

Colorway 2
Make 1

1. Lay out 2 light yellow A squares, 1 light teal A square, and 1 medium yellow A square as shown in colorway 1.

2. Sew the squares together in rows. Press the seams of each row to one side, alternating the direction with each row. Sew the rows together.

3. Repeat steps 1-2 to make a total of 4 Four-Patch Blocks in colorway 1.

4. Lay out the 2 dark yellow A squares, and 2 dark teal A squares as shown in colorway 2.

5. Sew the squares together in rows. Press the seams of each row to one side, alternating the direction with each row. Sew the rows together to make 1 Four-Patch Block in colorway 2.

Assembling the Quilt Center

1. Lay out the 16 Julia Blocks, 9 Friendship Star Blocks, 4 Quarter-Square Triangle Blocks, 17 Nine-Patch Blocks, 5 Four-Patch Blocks, 23 floral yellow 5" squares, 11 medium yellow 5" squares, 7 light yellow 5" squares, and 7 light teal 5" squares on a flat surface as shown in the *Sewing & Cutting Diagram*. Take care to place the blocks in the correct position to achieve the final quilt design.

2. Sew the blocks together into rows. Press the seams of each row to one side, alternating the direction with each row. Sew the rows together, adding the single block on the top row.

3. Press your quilt top with starch to prepare it for cutting. Referring to the *Sewing & Cutting Diagram*, use a pencil and ruler to mark the cutting lines and label the sections with arrows in the directions shown. Carefully cut the top into 3 sections on the pencil lines.

Note: Refer to page 9 if using the Cutting Guide and Arrow Guide Tape.

4. Lay out the sections as shown in the *Reassemble Diagram* with the arrows pointing down. Sew the sections together and press. Trim the excess fabric in the corners with a square up ruler to complete the quilt center.

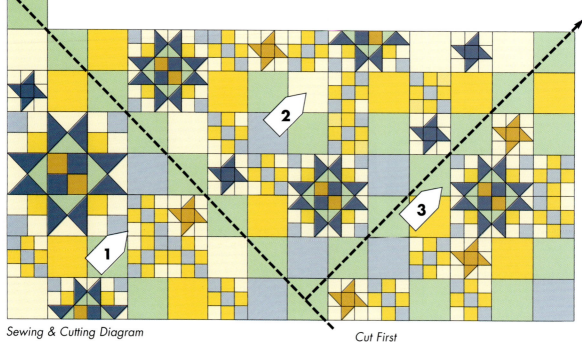

Sewing & Cutting Diagram

Cut First

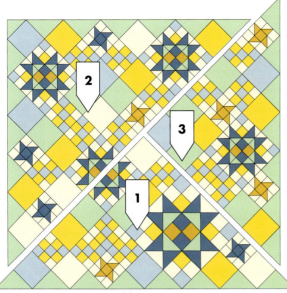

Reassemble Diagram

Adding the Borders

1. Sew the 1-1/2" dark yellow inner border strips together to make one long strip.

2. Measure your quilt center from top to bottom and cut two side border strips to size. Sew the borders to the side edges of the quilt center. Press seams toward the border.

3. Measure your quilt center from side to side and cut two top and bottom border strips to size. Sew the borders to the top and bottom edges of the quilt center. Press seams toward the border.

4. Sew the 2" dark teal outer border strips together to make one long strip.

5. Repeat steps 2-3 to measure and attach the dark teal outer border strips.

Finishing the Quilt

1. Sew the 56" x 29" backing rectangles together along one long edge, using a 1/2" seam allowance. Press the seam allowance open.

2. Layer the backing, batting, and the quilt top. Baste the layers together and hand- or machine-quilt as desired.

3. Use diagonal seams to sew the 2-1/2" wide binding strips together to make one long strip. Sew the binding to the edges of the quilt top.

4. Trim the extra batting and backing even with the edges of the quilt top. Turn the binding over the edge to the back and hand- or machine-sew in place.

Follow Your Star

Follow Your Star Quilt

Finished Size:
99" x 99"

Block Size:
9" square

Materials

2-1/4 yards dark teal fabric for blocks and borders

2-1/4 yards yellow floral fabric for blocks

2 yards dark yellow fabric for blocks and border corners

1-3/4 yards medium yellow fabric for blocks

2-1/2 yards light yellow fabric for blocks

1-1/2 yards light teal fabric for blocks

9 yards backing fabric

105" x 105" piece of batting

Cutting Instructions

From dark teal fabric, cut:
- (1) 10-1/4" x 40" strip.
  From the strip, cut: (2) 10-1/4" squares. Cut squares in quarters diagonally to make (8) A triangles for Quarter-Square Triangle Block.
- (2) 7-1/4" x 40" strips.
  From the strips, cut: (8) 7-1/4" squares. Cut squares in quarters diagonally to make (32) C triangles for Julia Block.
- (1) 5" x 40" strip.
  From the strip, cut: (2) 5" A squares for Four-Patch Block.
- (1) 3-7/8" x 40" strip.
  From the strip, cut: (8) 3-7/8" squares. Cut squares in half diagonally to make 16 B triangles for Friendship Star Blocks.
- (2) 3-1/2" x 40" strips.
  From the strips, cut: (12) 3-1/2" A squares for Julia Block and Friendship Star Block.
- (11) 3-1/2" x 40" strips for outer border.

From dark yellow fabric, cut:
- (1) 5" x 40" strip.
  From the strip, cut: (2) 5" A squares for Four-Patch Block.
- (1) 3-7/8" x 40" strip.
  From the strip, cut: (10) 3-7/8" squares. Cut squares in half diagonally to make 20 B triangles for Friendship Star Block.
- (2) 3-1/2" x 40" strips.
  From the strips, cut: (13) 3-1/2" A squares for Friendship Star Block and Julia Block.
- (10) 2-1/2" x 40" strips for inner border.
- (11) 2-1/2" x 40" strips for binding.

From yellow floral fabric. cut:
- (1) 10-1/4" x 40" strip.
  From the strip, cut: (1) 10-1/4" square. Cut square in quarters diagonally to make (4) A triangles for Quarter-Square Triangle Block.
- (6) 9-1/2" x 40" strips.
  From the strips, cut: (23) 9-1/2" squares.
- (2) 3-7/8" x 40" strips.

From the strips, cut: (16) 3-7/8" squares. Cut squares in half diagonally to make (32) B triangles for Julia Block.

From light teal fabric, cut:
- (2) 9-1/2" x 40" strip.
  From the strips, cut: (7) 9-1/2" squares.
- (1) 5" x 40" strip.
  From the strip, cut: (4) 5" A squares for Four-Patch Block
- (7) 3-1/2" x 40" strips.
  From the strips, cut: (67) 3-1/2" A squares for Nine-Patch Block and Julia Block.

From medium yellow fabric, cut:
- (3) 9-1/2" x 40" strips.
  From the strips, cut: (11) 9-1/2" squares.
- (1) 5" x 40" strip.
  From the strip, cut: (4) 5" A squares for Four-Patch Block
- (8) 3-1/2" x 40" strips.
  From the strips, cut: (84) 3-1/2" A squares for Nine-Patch Block and Julia Block.

From light yellow fabric, cut:
- (1) 10-1/4" x 40" strip.
  From the strip, cut: (1) 10-1/4" square. Cut square in quarters diagonally to make (4) A triangles for Quarter-Square Triangle Block.
- (2) 9-1/2" x 40" strips.
  From the strips, cut: (7) 9-1/2" squares.
- (1) 5" x 40" strip.
  From the strip, cut: (8) 5" A squares for Four-Patch Block.
- (4) 3-7/8" x 40" strips.
  From the strips, cut: (34) 3-7/8" squares. Cut squares in half diagonally to make (68) B triangles for Julia Block and Friendship Star Block.
- (10) 3-1/2" x 40" strips.
  From the strips, cut: (102) 3-1/2" A squares for Nine-Patch Block, Julia Block, and Friendship Star Block.

From backing fabric, cut:
- (3) 106" x 37" rectangles.

Finishing the Quilt

1. Sew the 37" x 106" backing rectangles together along one long edge, using a 1/2" seam allowance. Press the seam allowance open.

Follow Your Star

LABYRINTH

Pieced by Michele Parsons and Ruth Ellen Fise; hand quilted by Vicki Crawford

Finished Size:
51" x 62"

Block Size:
8" square

Materials
1-7/8 yards purple fabric for blocks, border and binding

1-5/8 yards pink fabric for blocks and border

1 yard dark gray fabric for blocks and border corners

3/4 yard light gray fabric for blocks and border corners

4 yards backing fabric

57" x 68" piece of batting

Refer to Square-agonals® Instructions and Sewing Tips on pages 7-10.

To make a 80" x 97" version of the Labyrinth quilt, refer to page 51 for Materials and Cutting Instructions.

Michelle Block   **Spiral Star Block**   **Pat Block**

Cutting Instructions

From purple fabric, cut:
- (3) 3-1/2" x 40" strips.
  From the strips, cut: (24) 3-1/2" squares. Cut the squares in half diagonally to make (48) A triangles for Spiral Star Block.
- (1) 3-1/4" x 40" strip.
  From the strip, cut: (10) 3-1/4" B squares for Pat Block.
- (7) 3-1/8" x 40" strips.
  From the strips, cut: (40) 3-1/8" x 5-7/8" A rectangles for Michelle Block.
- (1) 3-1/8" x 40" strip.
  From the strip, cut: (6) 3-1/8" B squares for Spiral Star Block.
- (6) 2-1/2" x 40" strips for binding.
- (6) 1-1/2" x 40" strips for inner border.

From pink fabric, cut:
- (3) 3-1/2" x 40" strips.
  From the strips, cut: (24) 3-1/2" squares. Cut the squares in half diagonally to make (48) A triangles for Spiral Star Block.
- (1) 3-1/4" x 40" strip.
  From the strip, cut: (8) 3-1/4" B squares for the Pat Block.
- (7) 3-1/8" x 40" strips.
  From the strips, cut: (40) 3-1/8" x 5-7/8" A rectangles for Michelle Block.
- (1) 3-1/8" x 40" strip.
  From the strip, cut: (6) 3-1/8" B squares for Spiral Star Block.
- (6) 2-1/2" x 40" strips for outer border.

From dark gray fabric, cut:
- (2) 8-1/2" x 40" strips.
  From the strips, cut: (6) 8-1/2" A squares for Pat Block.
- (3) 3-1/2" x 40" strips.
  From the strips, cut: (24) 3-1/2" squares. Cut the squares in half diagonally to make (48) A triangles for Spiral Star Block.
- (2) 1-7/8" x 40" strips.
  From the strips, cut: (40) 1-7/8" B squares for Michelle Block.
- (1) 1-1/2" x 40" strip.
  From the strip, cut: (8) 1-1/2" squares for border corner Four-Patch Block.

From light gray fabric, cut:
- (1) 8-1/2" x 40" strip.
  From the strip, cut: (3) 8-1/2" A squares for Pat Block.
- (3) 3-1/2" x 40" strips.
  From the strips, cut: (24) 3-1/2" A squares. Cut square in half diagonally to make (48) A triangles for Spiral Star Block.
- (2) 1-7/8" x 40" strips.
  From the strips, cut: (40) 1-7/8" B squares for Michelle Block.
- (1) 1-1/2" x 40" strip.
  From the strip, cut: (8) 1-1/2" squares for border corner Four-Patch Block.

From backing fabric, cut:
- (2) 57" x 35" rectangles.

Making the Michelle Block

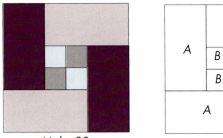 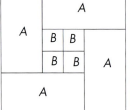

Make 20

1. Lay out 2 dark purple A rectangles, 2 pink A rectangles, 2 dark gray B squares, and 2 light gray B squares as shown.

2. Sew a dark gray B square and a light gray B square together. Repeat to make 2 pairs. Join the pairs together to make 1 four-patch unit.

3. With the left edges aligned, place a pink A rectangle along the top edge of the four-patch unit, right sides together. Sew the pieces together, beginning at the left edge and stopping approximately 1" from the top right corner of the four-patch unit.

4. Sew a purple A rectangle to the left edge of the unit from step 3. Add a pink A rectangle and purple A rectangle, continuing counter-clockwise around the four-patch unit.

5. Finish sewing the partial seam at the top of the four-patch unit to connect the pink and purple A rectangles and complete the block.

6. Repeat steps 1-5 to make a total of 20 Michelle Blocks.

Making the Spiral Star Block

Colorway 1 Make 6   *Colorway 2 Make 6*

1. Lay out 4 purple A triangles, 8 dark gray A triangles, 4 pink A triangles, and 1 purple B square as shown in colorway 1.

2. Sew a pink A triangle and a dark gray A triangle, right sides together, along the long edge to make a half-square triangle. Make a total of 4 pink/dark gray half-square triangles.

3. Sew a purple A triangle and a dark gray A triangle, right sides together, along the long edge to make a half-square triangle. Make a total of 4 purple/dark gray half-square triangles.

4. Lay out 4 pink/dark gray half-square triangles, 4 purple/dark gray half-square triangles, and 1 purple B square to form the Spiral Star Block.

5. Sew the pieces together in rows. Press the seams of each row to one side, alternating the direction with each row. Sew the rows together.

6. Repeat steps 1-5 to make a total of 6 Spiral Star Blocks in colorway 1.

7. Follow steps 1-5 to make 6 Spiral Star Blocks in colorway 2. Replace the dark gray A triangles with light gray A triangles, the purple A triangles with pink A triangles, the purple B square with pink B square, and the pink A triangles with purple A triangles.

Making the Pat Block

1. Lay out 1 dark gray A square and 2 pink B squares as shown in colorway 1.

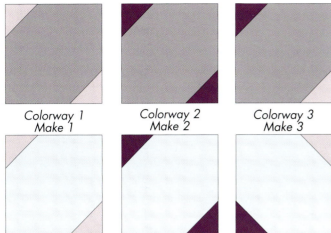

Colorway 1
Make 1

Colorway 2
Make 2

Colorway 3
Make 3

Colorway 4
Make 1

Colorway 5
Make 1

Colorway 6
Make 1

2. Draw a diagonal line on the wrong side of the pink B squares. With right sides together, place a pink square on the upper left corner of the dark gray A square. Sew on the diagonal line. Trim the seam allowance to 1/4" and press to form the corner triangle of the square.

3. With right sides together, add the second pink B square in the opposite corner of the dark gray A square. Sew on the diagonal line. Trim the seam allowance to 1/4" and press to form the corner triangle of the square.

4. Using the light and dark gray A squares and the pink and purple B squares, repeat steps 1-3 to make a total of 9 Pat Blocks in the colorways shown.

Making the Border Corner Four-Patch Block

1. Lay out 2 dark gray A squares and 2 light gray A squares as shown.

2. Sew a dark gray A square and a light gray B square together to make a pair. Repeat with the two remaining squares. Sew the pairs together to make a border corner Four-Patch block. Make a total of 4 border corner Four-Patch Blocks.

Assembling the Quilt Center

1. Lay out the 20 Michelle Blocks, 12 Spiral Star Blocks, and 9 Pat Blocks on a flat surface as shown in the *Sewing & Cutting Diagram*. Take care to place the blocks in the correct position to achieve the final quilt design.

2. Sew the blocks together into rows. Press the seams of each row to one side, alternating the direction with each row. Sew the rows together, adding the partial row on the top.

3. Press your quilt top with starch to prepare it for cutting. Referring to the *Sewing & Cutting Diagram*, use a pencil and ruler to mark the cutting lines and label the sections with arrows in the directions shown. Carefully cut the top into 3 sections on the pencil lines.

Note: Refer to page 9 if using the Cutting Guide and Arrow Guide Tape.

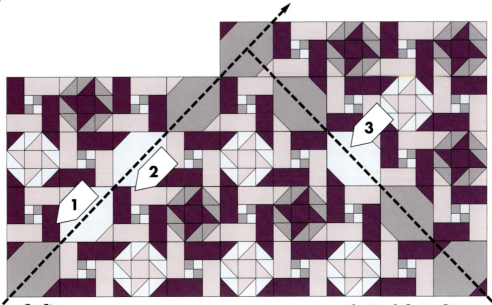

Cut First

Sewing & Cutting Diagram

4. Lay out the sections as shown in the *Reassemble Diagram* with the arrows pointing down. Sew the sections together and press. Trim the excess fabric in the corners with a square up ruler to complete the quilt center.

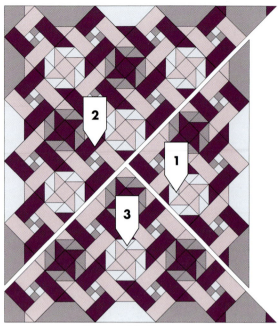

Reassemble Diagram

Adding the Borders

1. Sew the 1-1/2" purple inner border strips together to make one long strip.

2. Measure your quilt center from top to bottom and cut two side border strips to size. Sew the borders to the side edges of the quilt center. Press seams toward the border.

3. Measure your quilt center from side to side and cut two top and bottom border strips to size. Sew the borders to the top and bottom edges of the quilt center. Press seams toward the border.

4. Sew the 2-1/2" pink outer border strips together to make one long strip.

5. Measure your quilt center and cut four outer border strips to size. Sew the borders to the side edges of the quilt center. Press seams toward the inner border.

6. Sew a border corner Four-Patch Block to each end of the top and bottom borders. Sew these

borders to the top and bottom edges of the quilt center. Press seams toward the inner border.

Finishing the Quilt

1. Sew the 35" x 57" backing rectangles together along one long edge, using a 1/2" seam allowance. Press the seam allowance open.

2. Layer the backing, batting, and the quilt top. Baste the layers together and hand- or machine-quilt as desired.

3. Use diagonal seams to sew the 2-1/2" wide binding strips together to make one long strip. Sew the binding to the edges of the quilt top.

4. Trim the extra batting and backing even with the edges of the quilt top. Turn the binding over the edge to the back and hand- or machine-sew in place.

Labyrinth

Labyrinth

Finished Size:
80" x 97"

Block Size:
12" square

Materials

3-1/2 yards purple fabric
for blocks, border and binding

3-1/8 yards pink fabric
for blocks and border

1-1/2 yards dark gray fabric for
blocks and border corners

1-1/8 yards light gray fabric for
blocks and border corners

8-3/4 yards backing fabric

86" x 103" piece of batting

Cutting Instructions

From purple fabric, cut:

(3) 4-7/8" x 40" strips.
　　From the strips, cut: (24) 4-7/8" squares.
　　Cut the squares in half diagonally to make
　　(48) A triangles for Spiral Star Block.

(2) 4-5/8" x 40" strips.
　　From the strips, cut: (10) 4-5/8"
　　B squares for Pat Block.

(10) 4-1/2" x 40" strips.
　　From the strips, cut: (40) 4-1/2" x 8-1/2"
　　A rectangles for Michelle Block.

(1) 4-1/2" x 40" strip.
　　From the strip, cut: (6) 4-1/2"
　　B squares for Spiral Star Block.

(10) 2-1/2" x 40" strips for binding.

(9) 2-1/2" x 40" strips for inner border.

From pink fabric, cut:

(3) 4-7/8" x 40" strips.
　　From the strips, cut: (24) 4-7/8" squares.
　　Cut the squares in half diagonally to make
　　(48) A triangles for Spiral Star Block.

(1) 4-5/8" x 40" strip.
　　From the strip, cut: (8) 4-5/8"
　　B squares for the Pat Block.

(10) 4-1/2" x 40" strips.
　　From the strips, cut: (40) 4-1/2" x 8-1/2"
　　A rectangles for Michelle Block.

(1) 4-1/2" x 40" strip.
　　From the strip, cut: (6) 4-1/2"
　　B squares for Spiral Star Block.

(9) 4-1/2" x 40" strips for outer border.

From dark gray fabric, cut:

(2) 12-1/2" x 40" strips.
　　From the strips, cut: (6) 12-1/2"
　　A squares for Pat Block.

(3) 4-7/8" x 40" strips.
　　From the strips, cut: (24) 4-7/8" squares.
　　Cut the squares in half diagonally to make
　　(48) A triangles for Spiral Star Block.

(3) 2-1/2" x 40" strips.
　　From the strips, cut: (40) 2-1/2"
　　B squares for Michelle Block.

(1) 2-1/2" x 40" strip.
　　From the strip, cut: (8) 2-1/2" squares for
　　border corner Four-Patch Block.

From light gray fabric, cut:
- (1) 12-1/2" x 40" strip.
  From the strip, cut: (3) 12-1/2"
  A squares for Pat Block.
- (3) 4-7/8" x 40" strips.
  From the strips, cut: (24) 4-7/8" A squares.
  Cut square in half diagonally to make (48) A triangles for Spiral Star Block.
- (3) 2-1/2" x 40" strips.
  From the strips, cut: (40) 2-1/2"
  B squares for Michelle Block.
- (1) 2-1/2" x 40" strip.
  From the strip, cut: (8) 2-1/2" squares for border corner Four-Patch Block.

From backing fabric, cut:
- (3) 29" x 105" rectangles.

Adding the Borders

1. Sew the 2-1/2" purple inner border strips together to make one long strip.

2. Measure your quilt center from top to bottom and cut two side border strips to size. Sew the borders to the side edges of the quilt center. Press seams toward the border.

3. Measure your quilt center from side to side and cut two top and bottom border strips to size. Sew the borders to the top and bottom edges of the quilt center. Press seams toward the border.

4. Sew the 4-1/2" pink outer border strips together to make one long strip.

5. Measure your quilt center and cut four outer border strips to size. Sew the borders to the side edges of the quilt center. Press seams toward the inner border.

6. Sew a border corner Four-Patch Block to each end of the top and bottom borders. Sew these borders to the top and bottom edges of the quilt center. Press seams toward the inner border.

Finishing the Quilt

1. Sew the 29" x 105" backing rectangles together along one long edge, using a 1/2" seam allowance. Press the seam allowance open.

2. Layer the backing, batting, and the quilt top. Baste the layers together and hand- or machine-quilt as desired.

3. Use diagonal seams to sew the 2-1/2" wide binding strips together to make one long strip. Sew the binding to the edges of the quilt top.

4. Trim the extra batting and backing even with the edges of the quilt top. Turn the binding over the edge to the back and hand- or machine-sew in place.

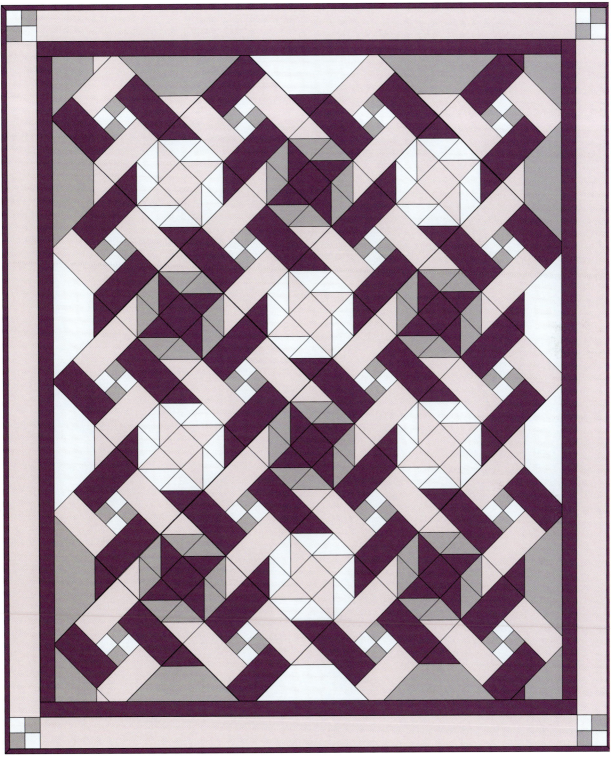

Labyrinth

SEASHELLS

Pieced by Stevie Robinson and Vicki Crawford; quilted by Finishing Touches Quilt Shop

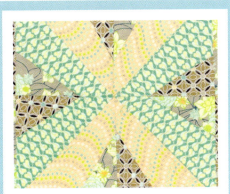

Finished Size:

50" x 63"

Block Size:

9" square

Materials

1-3/4 yards brown fabric for blocks and borders

2 -1/4 yards tan fabric for blocks and border

1-3/8 yards teal fabric for blocks

1/2 yard orange fabric for blocks

1/2 yard striped fabric for binding

4 yards backing fabric

56" x 69" piece of batting

*Refer to Square-agonals®
Instructions and Sewing Tips
on pages 7-10.*

Cutting Instructions

From brown fabric, cut:

(1) 9-1/2" x 40" strip.
   From the strip, cut: (2) 9-1/2" squares.

(4) 4-3/8" x 40" strips.
   From the strips, cut: (18) template E on page 60 for Stevie Block.

(1) 3-7/8" x 40" strip.
   From the strip, cut: (4) 3-7/8" squares. Cut the squares in half diagonally to make (8) triangles for border corner block.

(6) 3-1/2" x 40" border strips.

(2) 3-3/8" x 40" strips.
   From the strips, cut: (9) 3-3/8" x 5-3/8" rectangles. Cut the rectangles in half diagonally to make (18) G triangles for Stevie Block.

(1) 3-1/4" x 40" strip.
   From the strip, cut:
   (4) template C on page 58 for Stevie Block.

From tan fabric, cut:

(1) 9-1/2" x 40" strip.
   From the strip, cut: (4) 9-1/2" squares.

(4) 4-3/8" x 40" strips.
   From the strips, cut: (18) template B on page 60 for Stevie Block.

(1) 3-7/8" x 40" strip.
   From the strip, cut: (4) 3-7/8" squares. Cut squares in half diagonally to make (8) triangles for border corner blocks.

(6) 3-1/2" x 40" border strips.

(2) 3-3/8" x 40" strips.
   From the strips, cut: (9) 3-3/8" x 5-3/8" rectangles. Cut the rectangles in half diagonally to make (18) H triangles for Stevie Block.

(4) 3-1/4" x 40" strips.
   From the strips, cut:
   (18) template D on page 58 for Stevie Block.

From teal fabric, cut:

(1) 9-1/2" x 40" strip.
   From the strip, cut: (1) 9-1/2" square.
(11) 3-1/4" x 40" strips.
   From the strips, cut: (16) template A on
   page 59 and (16) template F on page 59
   for Stevie Block.

From orange fabric, cut:

(5) 3-1/4" x 40" strips.
   From the strips, cut: (14) template C on
   page 58, (2) template A on page 59, and
   (2) template F on page 59 for Stevie Block.

From striped fabric, cut:

(6) 2-1/2" x 40" binding strips.

From backing fabric, cut:

(2) 56" x 35" rectangles.

Making the Stevie Block

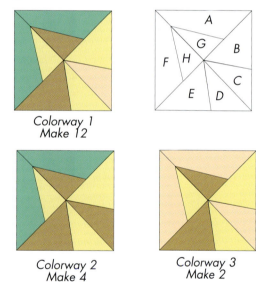

Colorway 1
Make 12

Colorway 2
Make 4

Colorway 3
Make 2

1. Lay out 1 each teal A and F piece, 1 each
   brown E and G piece, 1 each tan B, D,
   and H piece, and 1 orange C piece as shown
   in colorway 1. Mark all seam allowances for
   easy piecing.

2. Sew the teal A piece to the brown G piece,
   matching seam allowances. Sew the teal F piece
   to the tan H piece, matching seam allowances.
   Sew the A/G section and the F/H section
   together, matching seams and ends, to make half
   the Stevie block.

3. Sew a brown E piece to a tan D piece,
   matching seam allowances. Sew a tan B piece
   to the orange C piece, matching seam
   allowances. Sew the E/D section and the B/C
   section together, matching seams and ends to
   make half of the Stevie block.

4. Sew the 2 halves of the Stevie block
   together, matching seams and ends, to
   complete the block.

5. Repeat steps 1-4 to make a total of 12 Stevie
   Blocks in colorway 1.

6. Repeat steps 1-4 to make 4 Stevie Blocks in
   colorway 2. Replace the orange C piece
   with a brown C piece.

7. Repeat steps 1-4 to make 2 Stevie Blocks in
   colorway 3. Replace the teal A and F pieces
   with orange A and F pieces.

Making the Border Corner Block

1. Lay out 1 brown triangle and 1 tan
   triangle, as shown.

2. Sew the two triangles together to
   make the Border Corner Block.

3. Make a total of 8 Border Corner Blocks.

Assembling the Quilt Center

1. Lay out the 18 Stevie Blocks, 2 brown squares,
   and 4 tan squares on a flat surface as shown in
   the *Sewing & Cutting Diagram*. Take care to
   place the blocks in the correct position to
   achieve the final quilt design.

2. Sew the blocks together into rows. Press the
   seams of each row to one side, alternating the
   direction with each row. Sew the rows together,
   adding the partial row on the bottom.

3. Press your quilt top with starch to prepare it for
   cutting. Referring to the *Sewing & Cutting
   Diagram*, use a pencil and ruler to mark the
   cutting lines and label the sections with arrows in
   the directions shown. Carefully cut the top into 3
   sections on the pencil lines.

*Note: Refer to page 9 if using the Cutting
Guide and Arrow Guide Tape.*

4. Lay out the sections as shown in the *Reassemble Diagram* with the arrows pointing down. Sew the sections together and press. Trim the excess fabric in the corners with a square up ruler to complete the quilt center.

Adding the Borders

1. Sew together the 3-1/2" tan border strips to make one long strip.

2. Sew together the 3-1/2" brown border strips to make one long strip.

3. Measure your quilt center from top to bottom and cut two side border strips to size from the tan border strip. Sew the borders to the side edges of the quilt center. Press seams toward the borders.

4. Measure your quilt center from side to side and cut your top and bottom borders strips to size from the brown border strips.

5. Sew a Border Corner Block to each end of the top and bottom borders. Sew these borders to the top and bottom edges of the quilt center. Press seams toward the inner borders.

6. Repeat steps 1-5 for the outer border, using the brown strips on the sides and the tan strips on the top and bottom.

Finishing the Quilt

1. Sew the 35" x 56" backing rectangles together along one long edge, using a 1/2" seam allowance. Press the seam allowance open.

2. Layer the backing, batting, and the quilt top. Baste the layers together and hand- or machine-quilt as desired.

3. Use diagonal seams to sew the 2-1/2"-wide striped binding strips together to make one long strip. Sew the binding to the edges of the quilt top.

4. Trim the extra batting and backing even with the edges of the quilt top. Turn the binding over the edge to the back and hand- or machine-sew in place.

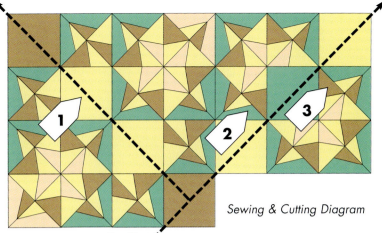

Sewing & Cutting Diagram

Cut First

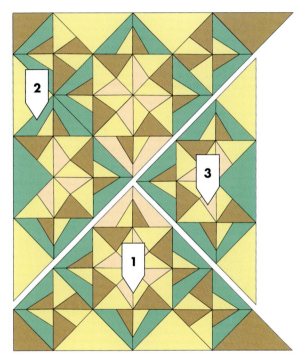

Reassemble Diagram

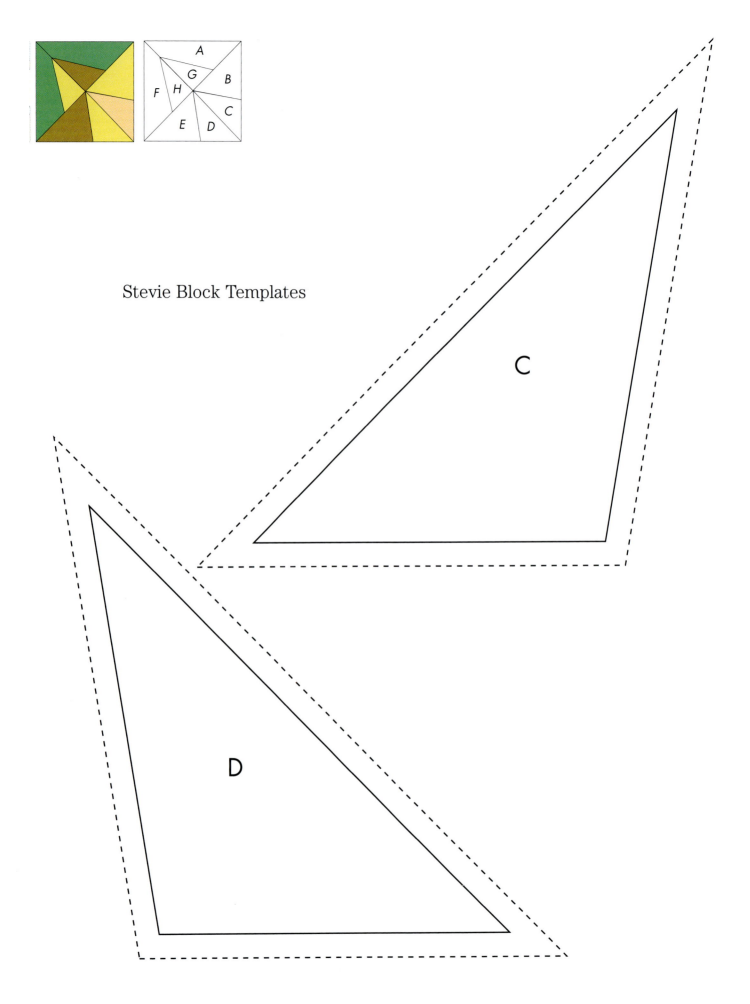

Stevie Block Templates

C

D

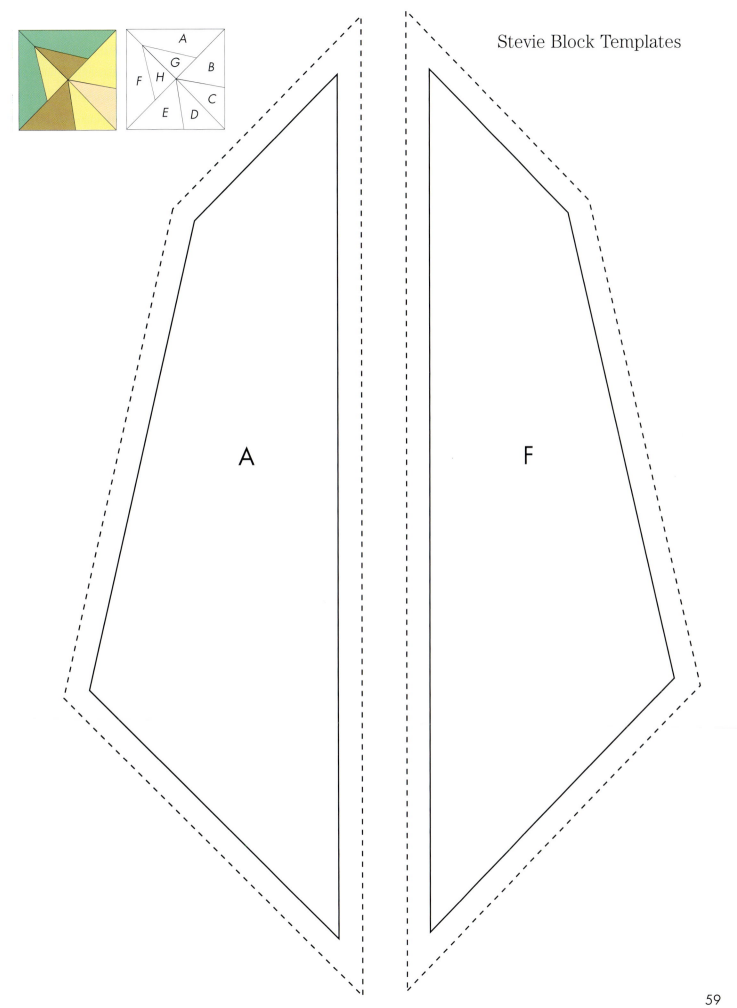

A

F

A
G
B
F H
E D
C

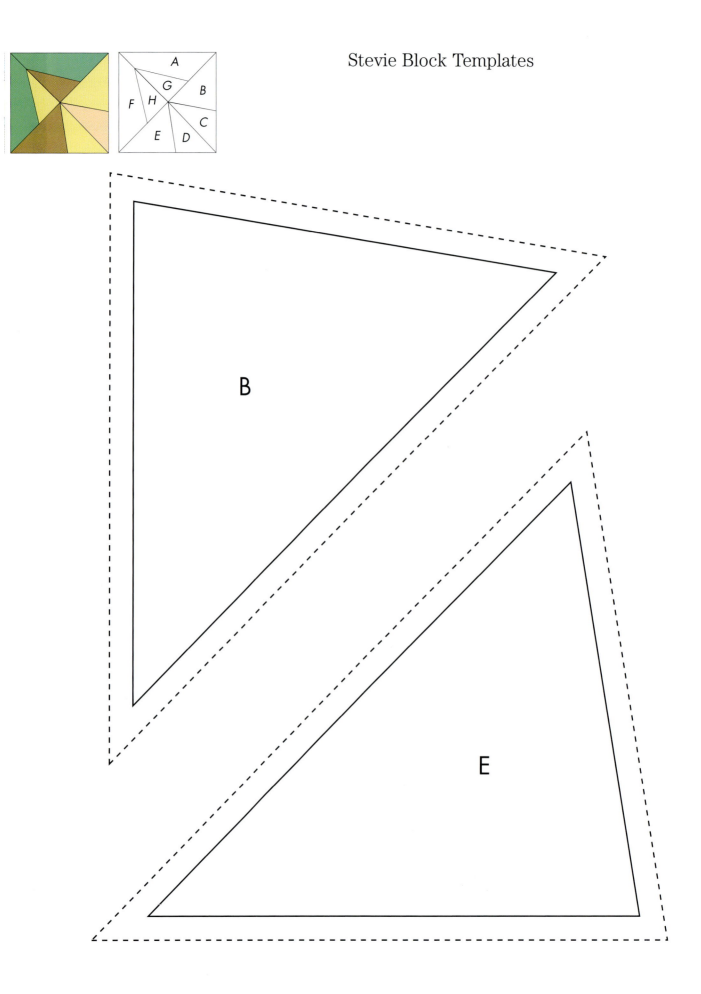

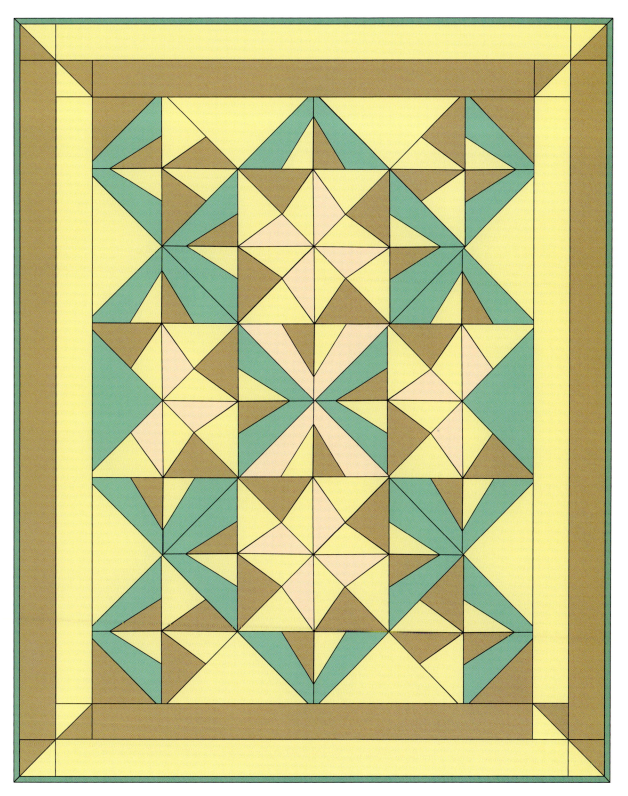

Seashells

BED OF LILACS

Pieced by Rachel Kerekes; quilted by Finishing Touches Quilt Shop

Finished Size:
71" x 85"

Block Size:
10" square

Materials

1 yard dark brown fabric for borders

1-7/8 yards large blue floral fabric for blocks and borders

1-1/2 yards purple fabric for blocks

1-7/8 yards gray fabric for blocks and borders

1-3/4 yards white floral fabric for blocks and borders

5/8 yard striped fabric for binding

5-1/4 yards backing fabric

77" x 91" piece of batting

Refer to Square-agonals® Instructions and Sewing Tips on pages 7-10.

Rachel Block    Flying Geese Block   Economy Patch Block

Cutting Instructions

From dark brown fabric, cut:
(2) 3" x 40" strips.
   From the strips, cut: (16) 3" B squares for Rachel Block.
(16) 1-1/2" x 40" strips for borders.

From large blue floral fabric, cut:
(4) 10-1/2" x 40" strip.
   From the strips, cut: (10) 10-1/2" squares.
(9) 2-1/2" x 40" strips for outer border.

From purple fabric, cut:
(3) 10-1/2" x 40" strips.
   From the strips, cut: (8) 10-1/2" squares.
(3) 5-7/8" x 40" strips.
   From the strips, cut: (14) 5-7/8" squares.
   Cut squares in half diagonally to make
   (28) A triangles for Flying Geese and Economy Blocks.

From gray fabric, cut:
(2) 10-1/2" x 40" strips.
   From the strips, cut: (6) 10-1/2" squares.
(3) 5-7/8" x 40" strips.
   From the strips, cut: (10) 5-7/8" squares.
   Cut squares in half diagonally to make
   (20) A triangles for Flying Geese and Rachel Blocks
   and cut (1) 5-1/2" C square for Economy Block.
(4) 3-1/2" x 40" strips.
   From the strips, cut: (4) 3-1/2" x 12" rectangles
   for top and bottom pieced inner borders.
   (6) 3-1/2" x 10-3/4" rectangles for side pieced
   inner borders.
   (4) 3-1/2" squares for border ends.
(2) 3" x 40" strips.
   From the strips, cut: (16) 3" B squares for Rachel Block.

From white floral fabric, cut:

(2) 10-1/2" x 40" strips.
  From the strips, cut: (6) 10-1/2" squares.
(2) 6-1/4" x 40" strips.
  From the strips, cut: (7) 6-1/4" squares.
  Cut squares in quarters to make
  (28) B triangles for Flying Geese
  and Economy Blocks.
(1) 5-7/8" x 40" strip.
  From the strip, cut: (4) 5-7/8" squares.
  Cut squares in half diagonally to make
  (8) A triangles for Rachel Block.
(5) 3-1/2" x 40" strips.
  From the strips, cut: (6) 3-1/2" x 12"
  rectangles for top and bottom pieced
  inner borders.
  (8) 3-1/2" x 10-3/4" rectangles
  for side pieced inner borders.

From striped fabric, cut:

(8) 2-1/2" x 40" binding strips.

From backing fabric, cut:

(2) 92" x 39" rectangles.

Making the Rachel Block

 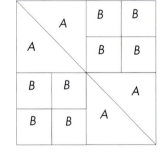

Make 4

1. Lay out 2 gray A triangles, 2 white floral A triangles, 4 dark brown B squares and 4 gray B squares, as shown.

2. Sew along the long edge of a gray A triangle and a white floral A triangle, right sides together, to make a half-square triangle. Make 2 gray/white floral half-square triangles.

3. Sew a dark brown B square and a gray B square together. Repeat to make 2 pairs. Sew the pairs together to make 1 four-patch unit. Make 2 four-patch units.

4. Arrange the 2 half-square triangles and the 2 four-patch units as shown in the Rachel Block. Sew the units together in rows. Sew the rows together.

5. Repeat steps 1-4 to make a total of 4 Rachel Blocks.

Making the Flying Geese Block

 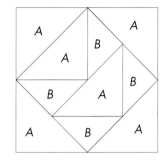

Make 6

1. Lay out 4 purple A triangles, 2 gray A triangles, and 4 white floral B triangles, as shown.

2. Sew a white floral B triangle to the side of a gray A triangle. Sew white floral B triangle to the opposite side of the gray A triangle to make a flying geese unit. Make 2 flying geese units.

3. Sew the 2 flying geese units together, as shown, to make the block center.

4. Sew 2 purple A triangles to opposite sides of the block center. Fold all pieces in half to mark the centers and match the centers when piecing. Complete the block by adding the remaining purple A triangles to the other 2 sides of the block center, matching center folds.

5. Repeat steps 1-4 to make a total of 6 Flying Geese Blocks.

Making the Economy Patch Block

 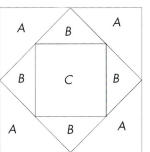

Make 1

1. Lay out a gray C square, 4 white floral B triangles and 4 purple A triangles, as shown.

2. Sew 2 white floral B triangles to opposite sides of the gray C square. Fold all pieces in half to mark the centers and match the centers when piecing. Sew the remaining white floral B triangles to the other 2 sides of the gray C square, matching center folds.

3. Repeat step 2 using the 4 purple A triangles to complete the Economy Patch Block.

Assembling the Quilt Center

1. Lay out the 4 Rachel Blocks, 6 Flying Geese Blocks, 1 Economy Block, 10 large blue floral squares, 8 purple squares, 6 gray squares, and 6 white floral squares on a flat surface as shown in the *Sewing & Cutting Diagram*. Take care to place the blocks in the correct position to achieve the final quilt design.

2. Sew the blocks together into rows. Press the seams of each row to one side, alternating the direction with each row. Sew the rows together, adding the partial row on the bottom.

3. Press your quilt top with starch to prepare it for cutting. Referring to the *Sewing & Cutting Diagram*, use a pencil and ruler to mark the cutting lines and label the sections with arrows in the directions shown. Carefully cut the top into 3 sections on the pencil lines.

Note: Refer to page 9 if using the Cutting Guide and Arrow Guide Tape.

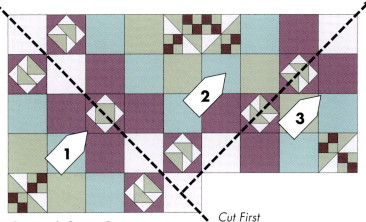

Sewing & Cutting Diagram   *Cut First*

4. Lay out the sections as shown in the *Reassemble Diagram* with the arrows pointing down. Sew the sections together and press. Trim the excess fabric in the corners with a square up ruler to complete the quilt center.

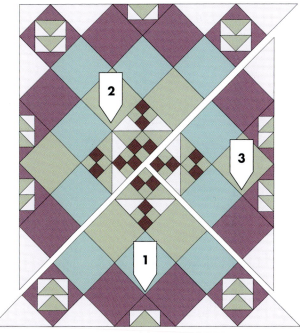

Reassemble Diagram

Adding the Border

1. Sew (4) 3-1/2" x 10-3/4" white floral rectangles and (3) 3-1/2" x 10-3/4" gray rectangles together, end to end, alternating the colors to make a side border. Make 2 side borders.

Make 2

2. Sew (3) 3-1/2" x 12" white floral rectangles and (2) 3-1/2" x 12" gray rectangles together, end to end, alternating the colors to make a top/bottom border. Make 2 top/bottom borders.

Make 2

3. Sew the 1-1/2" dark brown border strips together to make one long strip. Cut (4) 1-1/2" x 3-1/2" pieces for border ends. Set these pieces aside.

4. Measure your quilt center from top to bottom and cut 2 dark brown border strips to size. Cut the 2 side borders to the same size, measuring from the center out so the rectangle design is centered. Sew a dark brown strip to one side of each pieced side border strip. *Do not sew the borders on the quilt center yet.*

5. Measure your quilt center from side to side and cut the top/bottom border strips to size, measuring from the center out so the rectangle design is centered. Add a dark brown 1-1/2" x 3-1/2" border end to each end of the top/bottom border strip. Add a 3-1/2" gray square to the end of each top/bottom border strip. This completes the top and bottom borders.

6. Sew the side borders to the side edges of the quilt center, with the dark brown border next to the quilt center top. Press seams toward the outer border.

7. Re-measure the quilt center from side to side and cut (2) 1-1/2" dark brown border strips to this size for the top and bottom. Sew these to the top and bottom edges of the quilt center. Press seams toward the outer border.

8. Sew the top/bottom border strips to the top and bottom edges of the quilt center. Press seams toward the outer borders.

9. Measure your quilt center from top to bottom and cut (2) 1-1/2" dark brown border strips to this size for the sides. Sew the borders to the side edges of the quilt center. Press seams toward the outer border.

10. Measure your quilt center again from side to side and cut (2) 1-1/2" dark brown top and bottom border strips to size. Sew the borders to the top/bottom of the quilt center. Press seams toward the outer border.

11. Sew the 2-1/2" large blue floral border strips together to make one long strip

12. Repeat steps 9-10 to measure and add the large blue floral outer borders.

Finishing the Quilt

1. Sew the 39" x 92" backing rectangles together along one long edge, using a 1/2" seam allowance. Press the seam allowance open.

2. Layer the backing, batting, and the quilt top. Baste the layers together and hand- or machine-quilt as desired.

3. Use diagonal seams to sew the 2-1/2" wide striped binding strips together to make one long strip. Sew the binding to the edges of the quilt top.

4. Trim the extra batting and backing even with the edges of the quilt top. Turn the binding over the edge to the back and hand- or machine-sew in place.

Bed of Lilacs

STRAWBERRY FIELDS

Pieced by Krujetta Clark; quilted by Finishing Touches Quilt Shop

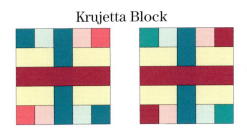

Krujetta Block

Finished Size:
80" x 80"

Block Size:
12" square

Materials
1-5/8 yards dark teal fabric for blocks and borders

1 yard medium teal fabric for blocks and borders

5/8 yard light teal fabric for blocks

1-5/8 yards dark pink fabric for blocks and borders

1 yard medium pink fabric for blocks and borders

5/8 yard light pink for blocks

1-5/8 yards white print fabric for blocks

5/8 yard striped fabric for binding

7-1/2 yards backing fabric

86" x 86" piece of batting

*Refer to Square-agonals®
Instructions and Sewing Tips
on pages 7-10.*

Cutting Instructions

From dark teal fabric, cut:
(14) 2-7/8" x 40" strips.
From the strips, cut: (32) 2-7/8" A squares for Krujetta Block, (66) 2-7/8" x 5-1/4" B rectangles for Krujetta Block and (4) 2-1/2" border corner squares.
(9) 1-1/2" x 40" strips.
From the strips, cut: (64) 1-1/2" x 5" rectangles for middle borders.
(1) 1-1/8" x 40" strip.
From the strip, cut: (20) 1-1/8" squares for Border Corner Nine-Patch Blocks.

From medium teal fabric, cut:
(3) 2-7/8" x 40" strips.
From the strips, cut: (34) 2-7/8" A squares for Krujetta Block.
(9) 2-1/2" x 40" strips for outer border.

From light teal fabric, cut:
(6) 2-7/8" x 40" strips.
From the strips, cut: (66) 2-7/8" A squares for Krujetta Block.

From dark pink fabric, cut:
(14) 2-7/8" x 40" strips.
From the strips, cut: (34) 2-7/8" A squares for Krujetta Block, (33) 2-7/8" x 12-1/2" C rectangles for Krujetta Block and (4) 2-1/2" border corner squares.
(9) 1-1/2" x 40" strips.
From the strips, cut: (64) 1-1/2" x 5" rectangles for middle borders.
(1) 1-1/8" x 40" strip.
From the strip, cut: (16) 1-1/8" squares for Border Corner Nine-Patch Blocks.

From medium pink fabric, cut:
(3) 2-7/8" x 40" strips.
From the strips, cut: (32) 2-7/8" A squares for Krujetta Block.
(9) 2-1/2" x 40" strips for inner border.

From light pink fabric, cut:
(6) 2-7/8" x 40" strips.
From the strips, cut: (66) 2-7/8"
A squares for Krujetta Block.

From white print fabric, cut:
(19) 2-7/8" x 40" strips.
From the strips, cut: (132) 2-7/8" x 5-1/4"
B rectangles for Krujetta Blocks.

From striped fabric, cut:
(9) 2-1/2" x 40" binding strips.

From backing fabric, cut:
(3) 30" x 86" rectangles.

Making the Krujetta Block

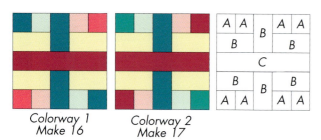

Colorway 1
Make 16

Colorway 2
Make 17

1. Lay out 2 dark teal A squares, 2 light teal A squares, 2 medium pink A squares, 2 light pink A squares, 4 white print B rectangles, 2 dark teal B rectangles, and 1 dark pink C rectangle as shown in colorway 1.

2. Sew a dark teal square and a light teal A square together. Repeat to make 2 pairs. Sew a pair to the top of a white print B rectangle, with the dark teal on the top left to make a teal corner block. Make 2 teal corner blocks.

3. Sew a medium pink A square and a light pink A square together. Repeat to make 2 pairs. Sew a pair to the top of a white print B rectangle, with the light pink on the top left to make a pink corner block. Make 2 pink corner blocks.

4. Sew a teal corner block and a pink corner block to opposite sides of a dark teal B rectangle to make a block half. Make 2 block halves.

5. Sew the two block halves on opposite sides of a dark pink C rectangle to complete the block.

6. Repeat steps 1-5 to make a total of 16 Krujetta Blocks in colorway 1.

7. Follow steps 1-5 to make a total of 17 Krujetta Blocks in colorway 2. Replace the dark teal A squares with medium teal A squares and replace the medium pink A squares with dark pink A squares.

Assembling the Quilt Center

1. Lay out the 33 Krujetta Blocks on a flat surface as shown in the *Sewing & Cutting Diagram*. Take care to place the blocks in the correct position to achieve the final quilt design.

2. Sew the blocks together into rows. Press the seams of each row to one side, alternating the direction with each row. Sew the rows together, adding the single block to the top row.

3. Press your quilt top with starch to prepare it for cutting. Referring to the *Sewing & Cutting Diagram*, use a pencil and ruler to mark the cutting lines and label the sections with arrows in the directions shown. Carefully cut the top into 3 sections on the pencil lines.

Note: Refer to page 9 if using the Cutting Guide and Arrow Guide Tape.

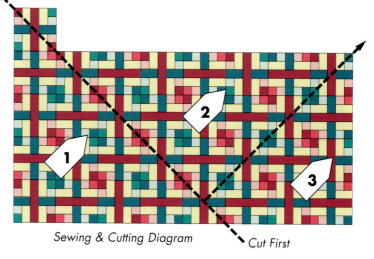

Sewing & Cutting Diagram   *Cut First*

4. Lay out the sections as shown in the *Reassemble Diagram* with the arrows pointing down. Sew the sections together and press. Trim the excess fabric in the corners with a square up ruler to complete the quilt center.

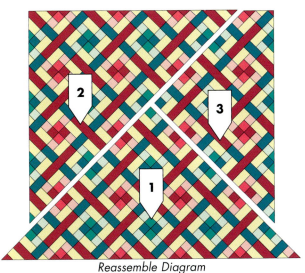

Reassemble Diagram

Making the Border Corner Nine-Patch Block

1. Lay out 5 dark teal squares and 4 dark pink squares, as shown.

2. Sew the squares into rows. Press the seams of each row to one side, alternating the direction with each row. Sew the rows together.

3. Repeat steps 1-2 to make a total of 4 Border Corner Nine-Patch Blocks.

Adding the Inner Border

1. Sew the 2-1/2" medium pink border strips together to make one long strip.

2. Measure your quilt center and cut 4 border strips to size from the medium pink border strip. Sew the borders to the left and right edges of the quilt center. Press seams toward the border.

3. Sew a dark pink 2-1/2" square to each end of the top and bottom borders. Sew the borders to the top and bottom edges of the quilt center. Press seams toward the border.

Adding the Middle Border

1. Sew a 1-1/2" x 5-1/2" dark teal rectangle and a 1-1/2" x 5-1/2" dark pink rectangle together along one long edge to make a pair. Make (64) pairs.

Make 64

2. Sew 16 pairs together, end to end along the short edge and alternating the colors, to make a middle border strip. Make 4 middle border strips.

Make 4

3. Measure your quilt center and cut 4 middle border strips to size from the pieced dark teal/dark pink border strip, measuring from the center out so the pieced design is centered. Sew the borders to the left and right edges of the quilt center. Press seams toward the inner border.

4. Sew a border corner Nine-Patch Block to each end of the top and bottom borders. Sew the borders to the top and bottom edges of the quilt center. Press seams toward the inner border.

Adding the Outer Border

1. Sew the 2-1/2" medium teal border strips together to make one long strip.

2. Measure your quilt center and cut 4 border strips to size from the medium teal border strip. Sew the borders to the left and right edges of the quilt center. Press seams toward the outer border. Sew a dark teal 2-1/2" square to each end of the top and bottom borders. Sew the borders to the top and bottom edges of the quilt center. Press seams toward the outer border.

Finishing the Quilt

1. Sew the (3) 30" x 86" backing rectangles together along the long edges, using a 1/2" seam allowance. Press the seam allowances open.

2. Layer the backing, batting, and the quilt top. Baste the layers together and hand- or machine-quilt as desired.

3. Use diagonal seams to sew the 2-1/2" wide striped binding strips together to make one long strip. Sew the binding to the edges of the quilt top.

4. Trim the extra batting and backing even with the edges of the quilt top. Turn the binding over the edge to the back and hand- or machine-sew in place.

Strawberry Fields

APPLE TREE

Pieced by Debbie Carpino, Michelle Parsons, and Stevie Robinson;
quilted by Finishing Touches Quilt Shop

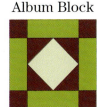

Debbie Block　　**Twila Block**　　**Album Block**

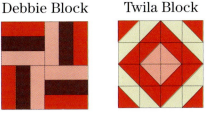

Finished Size:
80" x 80"

Block Size:
12" square

Materials
2-5/8 yards brown fabric for blocks, borders, and binding

2-1/4 yards red fabric for blocks and borders

1-1/2 yards pink fabric for blocks and borders

1-1/4 yards green fabric for blocks and borders

1-1/4 yards white print fabric for blocks

7-1/2 yards backing fabric

86" x 86" piece of batting

*Refer to Square-agonals®
Instructions and Sewing Tips
on pages 7-10.*

Cutting Instructions

From brown fabric, cut:
(2) 4-1/2" x 40" strips.
　　From the strips, cut: (16) 4-1/2" C squares for Album Block.
(1) 3-1/2" x 40" strip.
　　From the strip, cut: (16) 3-1/2" x 2" B rectangles for
　　Border Corner Album Block.
(3) 2-7/8" x 40" strip.
　　From the strip, cut: (32) 2-7/8" A squares for Album Block.
(9) 2-1/2" x 40" strips.
　　From the strips, cut: (52) 2-1/2" x 6-1/2" A rectangles for
　　Debbie Block.
(9) 2-1/2" x 40" binding strips.
(9) 2" x 40" strips for borders.

From red fabric, cut:
(10) 3-7/8" x 40" strips.
　　From the strips, cut: (96) 3-7/8" squares. Cut the squares in
　　half diagonally to make (192) A triangles for Twila Block.
(9) 2-1/2" x 40" strips.
　　From the strips, cut: (52) 2-1/2" x 6-1/2" A rectangles for
　　Debbie Block.
(9) 2" x 40" strips for borders.

From pink fabric, cut:
(3) 3-7/8" x 40" strips.
　　From the strips, cut: (24) 3-7/8" squares. Cut the squares in
　　half diagonally to make (48) A triangles for Twila Block.
(9) 2-1/2" x 40" strips.
　　From the strips, cut: (52) 2-1/2" x 6-1/2" A rectangles for
　　Debbie Block.
(9) 2" x 40" strips for borders.

From green fabric, cut:
- (7) 2-7/8" x 40" strips.
  From the strips, cut: (32) 2-7/8" x 7-3/4" B rectangles for Album Block.
- (1) 2-3/8" x 40" strip.
  From the strip, cut: (8) 2-3/8" squares. Cut the squares in half diagonally to make (16) C triangles for Border Corner Album Block.
- (1) 2" x 40" strip.
  From the strip, cut: (16) 2" A squares for Border Corner Album Block.
- (9) 2" x 40" strips for borders.

From white print fabric, cut:
- (2) 5-5/8" x 40" strips.
  From the strips, cut: (8) 5-5/8" D squares for Album Block and (4) 2-5/8" D squares for Border Corner Album Block.
- (8) 3-7/8" x 40" strips.
  From the strip, cut: (72) 3-7/8" squares. Cut the squares in half diagonally to make (144) A triangles for Twila Block.

From backing fabric, cut:
- (3) 30" x 90" rectangles.

Making the Debbie Block

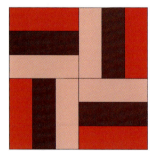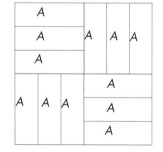

Make 13

1. Lay out 4 red A rectangles, 4 brown A rectangles, and 4 pink A rectangles, as shown.

2. Sew a red A rectangle and a pink A rectangle to opposite sides of a brown A rectangle, along the long edge, to make 1 corner unit. Make 4 corner units.

3. Sew the corner units together in pairs, rotating the units so the pink strips meet to make a block half. Make 2 block halves.

4. Sew the 2 block halves together to complete the block.

5. Repeat steps 1-4 to make a total of 13 Debbie Blocks.

Making the Twila Block

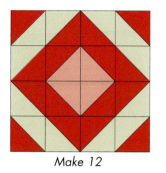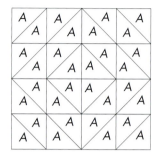

Make 12

1. Lay out 16 red A triangles, 12 white print A triangles, and 4 pink A triangles as shown.

2. Sew a red A triangle and a white print A triangle together along the long edge to make a half-square triangle. Make 12 red/white print half-square triangles.

3. Sew a red A triangle and a pink A triangle together along the long edge to make a half-square triangle. Make 4 red/pink half-square triangles.

4. Arrange the half-square triangles as shown in the Twila Block. Sew the blocks together in rows. Press the seams of each row to one side, alternating the direction with each row.

5. Sew the rows together to complete the block.

6. Repeat steps 1-5 to make a total of 12 Twila Blocks.

Making the Album Block

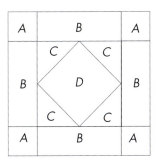

Make 8

Note: Refer to page 9 if using the Cutting Guide and Arrow Guide Tape.

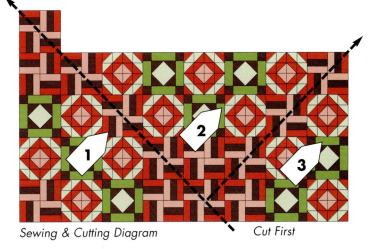

1. Lay out 4 brown A squares, 4 brown C triangles, 4 green B rectangles, and (1) 5-5/8" white print D square, as shown.

2. Sew 2 brown C triangles to opposite sides of the white print D square. Sew the 2 remaining brown C triangles to the remaining sides of the square to make the center block unit.

3. Sew 2 green B rectangles to opposite sides of the center block unit.

4. Sew a brown A square to each end of the remaining green B rectangles. Sew the green/brown strips to opposite sides of the center block unit to complete the block.

5. Repeat steps 1-4 to make a total of 8 Album Blocks.

Assembling the Quilt Center

1. Lay out the 13 Debbie Blocks, 12 Twila Blocks, and 8 Album Blocks on a flat surface as shown in the *Sewing & Cutting Diagram*. Take care to place the blocks in the correct position to achieve the final quilt design.

2. Sew the blocks together into rows. Press the seams of each row to one side, alternating the direction with each row. Sew the rows together, adding the single block to the top row.

3. Press your quilt top with starch to prepare it for cutting. Referring to the *Sewing & Cutting Diagram*, use a pencil and ruler to mark the cutting lines and label the sections with arrows in the directions shown. Carefully cut the top into 3 sections on the pencil lines.

Sewing & Cutting Diagram   **Cut First**

4. Lay out the sections as shown in the *Reassemble Diagram* with the arrows pointing down. Sew the sections together and press. Trim the excess fabric in the corners with a square up ruler to complete the quilt center.

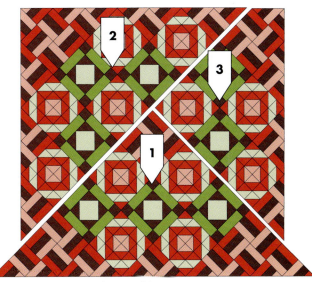

Reassemble Diagram

Making the Border Corner

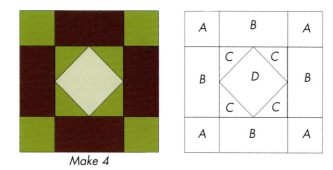

Make 4

Album Block

1. Lay out 4 green A squares, 4 green C triangles, 4 brown B rectangles, and (1) 2-5/8 white print D square as shown.

2. Sew 2 green C triangles to opposite sides of the white print D square. Sew the 2 remaining green C triangles to the remaining sides of the square to make the center block unit.

3. Sew 2 brown B rectangles to opposite sides of the center block unit.

4. Sew a green A square to each end of the remaining brown B rectangles. Sew the green/brown strips to opposite sides of the center block unit to complete the block.

5. Repeat steps 1-4 to make a total of 4 Border Corner Album Blocks.

Adding the Borders

1. Sew the 2" brown border strips together to make one long strip. Repeat with the 2" red strips, 2" pink strips, and 2" green strips.

2. Sew the pink, green, red, and brown strips from step 1 together along the long edges, following the color order given. Press seams toward the pink strip. These sewn strips will be treated as one border strip.

3. Measure your quilt center and cut 4 border strips to size. Sew the borders to the left and right edges of the quilt center with the brown strip against the quilt center. Press seams toward the pink border.

4. Sew a Border Corner Album Blocks to each end of the top and bottom border strip. Sew these borders to the top and bottom edges of the quilt center with the brown strip against the quilt center. Press seams toward the pink border.

Finishing the Quilt

1. Sew the (3) 30" x 90" backing rectangles together along the long edges, using a 1/2" seam allowance. Press the seam allowances open.

2. Layer the backing, batting, and the quilt top. Baste the layers together and hand- or machine-quilt as desired.

3. Use diagonal seams to sew the 2-1/2" wide brown binding strips together to make one long strip. Sew the binding to the edges of the quilt top.

4. Trim the extra batting and backing even with the edges of the quilt top. Turn the binding over the edge to the back and hand- or machine-sew in place.

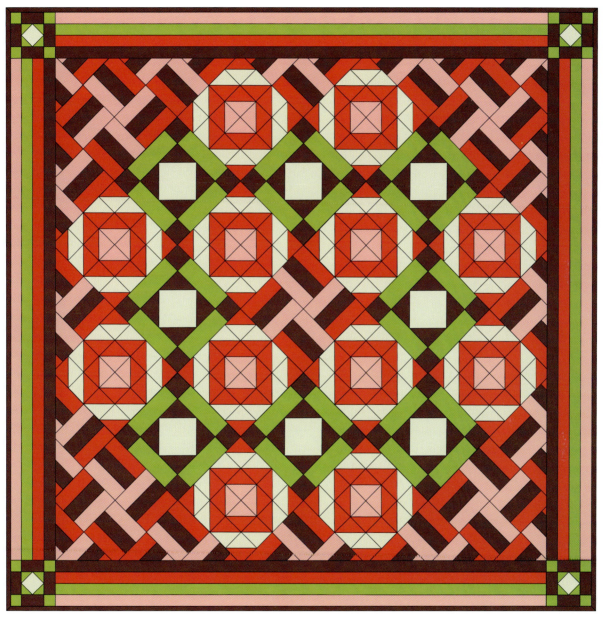

Apple Tree

SUPER NOVA

Pieced by Stevie Robinson, Judy Beveridge, Vicki Crawford, Julia Plunkett;
quilted by Finishing Touches Quilt Shop

Finished Size:
82" x 98"

Block Size:
12" square

Materials
1 yard dark purple fabric for blocks and border

7/8 yard medium purple fabric
for blocks and border

3/4 yard light purple fabric
for blocks and border

7/8 yard dark pink fabric for blocks and border

7/8 yard medium pink fabric
for blocks and border

3/4 yard light pink fabric for blocks and border

7/8 yard dark orange fabric
for blocks and border

7/8 yard medium orange fabric
for blocks and border

3/4 yard light orange fabric
for blocks and border

1 yard dark yellow fabric for blocks and border

7/8 yard medium yellow for blocks and border

3/4 yard light yellow fabric
for blocks and border

1-7/8 yards dark blue fabric
for blocks, border, and binding

7/8 yard medium blue fabric
for blocks and border

5/8 yard light blue fabric for blocks and border

8-7/8 yards backing fabric

88" x 106" piece of batting

*Refer to Square-agonals® Instructions
and Sewing Tips on pages 7-10.*

Double Star Block   Border Star Block   Border Corner Block

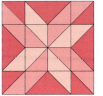  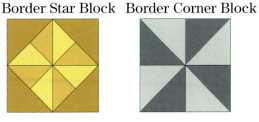

Cutting Instructions

From dark purple fabric, cut:
(2) 7-1/4" x 40" strips.
  From the strips, cut: (8) 7-1/4" squares.
  Cut the squares in quarters diagonally to make
  (32) B triangles for Double Star Block and
  (2) 3-1/2" x 6-1/2" rectangles
  for border ends.

(5) 3-7/8" x 40" strips.
  From the strips, cut: (44) 3-7/8" squares.
  Cut the squares in half diagonally to make
  (88) A triangles for Double Star Block and
  Border Star Block.

From medium purple fabric, cut:

(2) 4-1/4" x 40" strips.

> From the strips, cut: (14) 4-1/4" squares.
> Cut the squares in quarters diagonally to make
> (56) B triangles for Border Star Block.

(5) 3-7/8" x 40" strips.

> From the strips, cut: (48) 3-7/8" squares.
> Cut the squares in half diagonally to make
> (96) A triangles for Double Star Block.

From light purple fabric, cut:

(2) 4-1/4" x 40" strips.

> From the strips, cut: (14) 4-1/4" squares.
> Cut the squares in quarters diagonally to make
> (56) B triangles for Border Star Block.

(4) 3-7/8" x 40" strips.

> From the strips, cut: (32) 3-7/8" squares.
> Cut the squares in half diagonally to make
> (64) A triangles for Double Star Block.

From dark pink fabric, cut:

(2) 7-1/4" x 40" strips.

> From the strips, cut: (8) 7-1/4" squares.
> Cut the squares in quarters diagonally to make
> (32) B triangles for Double Star Block.
> (2) 3-1/2" x 6-1/2" rectangles for
> border ends.

(4) 3-7/8" x 40" strips.

> From the strips, cut: (38) 3-7/8" squares.
> Cut the squares in half diagonally to make
> (76) A triangles for Double Star Block and
> Border Star Block.

From medium pink fabric, cut:

(2) 4-1/4" x 40" strips.

> From the strips, cut: (11) 4-1/4" squares.
> Cut the squares in quarters diagonally to make
> (44) B triangles for Border Star Block.

(5) 3-7/8" x 40" strips.

> From the strips, cut: (48) 3-7/8" squares.
> Cut the squares in half diagonally to make
> (96) A triangles for Double Star Block.

From light pink fabric, cut:

(2) 4-1/4" x 40" strips.

> From the strips, cut: (11) 4-1/4" squares.
> Cut the squares in quarters diagonally to make
> (44) B triangles for Border Star Block.

(4) 3-7/8" x 40" strips.

> From the strips, cut: (32) 3-7/8" squares.
> Cut the squares in half diagonally to make
> (64) A triangles for Double Star Block.

From dark orange fabric, cut:

(2) 7-1/4" x 40" strips.

> From the strips, cut: (8) 7-1/4" squares.
> Cut the squares in quarters diagonally to make
> (32) B triangles for Double Star Block.
> (2) 3-1/2" x 6-1/2" rectangles for
> border ends.

(4) 3-7/8" x 40" strips.

> From the strips, cut: (38) 3-7/8" squares.
> Cut the squares in half diagonally to make
> (76) A triangles for Double Star Block and
> Border Star Block.

From medium orange fabric, cut:

(2) 4-1/4" x 40" strips.

> From the strips, cut: (11) 4-1/4" squares.
> Cut the squares in quarters diagonally to make
> (44) B triangles for Border Star Block.

(5) 3-7/8" x 40" strips.

> From the strips, cut: (48) 3-7/8" squares.
> Cut the squares in half diagonally to make
> (96) A triangles for Double Star Block.

From light orange fabric, cut:

(2) 4-1/4" x 40" strips.

> From the strips, cut: (11) 4-1/4" squares.
> Cut the squares in quarters diagonally to make
> (44) B triangles for Border Star Block.

(4) 3-7/8" x 40" strips.

> From the strips, cut: (32) 3-7/8" squares.
> Cut the squares in half diagonally to make
> (64) A triangles for Double Star Block.

From dark yellow fabric, cut:

(2) 7-1/4" x 40" strips.
  From the strips, cut: (8) 7-1/4" squares. Cut the squares in quarters diagonally to make (32) B triangles for Double Star Block and (2) 3-1/2" x 6-1/2" rectangles for border ends.

(5) 3-7/8" x 40" strips.
  From the strips, cut: (44) 3-7/8" squares. Cut the squares in half diagonally to make (88) A triangles for Double Star Block and Border Star Block.

From medium yellow fabric, cut:

(2) 4-1/4" x 40" strips.
  From the strips, cut: (14) 4-1/4" squares. Cut the squares in quarters diagonally to make (56) B triangles for Border Star Block.

(5) 3-7/8" x 40" strips.
  From the strips, cut: (48) 3-7/8" squares. Cut the squares in half diagonally to make (96) A triangles for Double Star Block.

From light yellow fabric, cut:

(2) 4-1/4" x 40" strips.
  From the strips, cut: (14) 4-1/4" squares. Cut the squares in quarters diagonally to make (56) B triangles for Border Star Block.

(4) 3-7/8" x 40" strips.
  From the strips, cut: (32) 3-7/8" squares. Cut the squares in half diagonally to make (64) A triangles for Double Star Block.

From dark blue fabric, cut:

(2) 7-1/4" x 40" strips.
  From the strips, cut: (9) 7-1/4" squares. Cut the squares in quarters diagonally to make (36) B triangles for Double Star Block.

(2) 3-7/8" x 40" strips.
  From the strips, cut: (18) 3-7/8" squares. Cut the squares in half diagonally to make (36) A triangles for Double Star Block.

(10) 2-1/2" x 40" binding strips.

(9) 1-1/2" x 40" strips for inner border.

From medium blue fabric, cut:

(7) 3-7/8" x 40" strips.
  From the strips, cut: (62) 3-7/8" squares. Cut the squares in half diagonally to make (124) A triangles for Double Star Block and Border Corner Block.

From light blue fabric, cut:

(5) 3-7/8" x 40" strips.
  From the strips, cut: (44) 3-7/8" squares. Cut the squares in half diagonally to make (88) A triangles for Double Star Block and Border Corner Block.

From backing fabric, cut:

(3) 30" x 106" rectangles.

Making the Double Star Block

Pink Colorway Make 8

Orange Colorway Make 8

Purple Colorway Make 8

Yellow Colorway Make 8

Blue Colorway Make 9

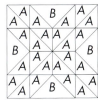

1. Lay out 4 dark blue A triangles, 4 dark blue B triangles, 12 medium blue A triangles, and 8 light blue A triangles as shown.

2. Sew a dark blue A triangle and a medium blue A triangle together along the long edge to make a half-square triangle. Make 4 dark/medium blue half-square triangles.

3. Sew a medium blue A triangle and a light blue A triangle together along the long edge to make a half-square triangle. Make 4 medium/light blue half-square triangles.

4. Sew a light blue A triangle to the right side of a dark blue B triangle. Sew a *medium* blue A triangle to the *left* side of the dark blue B triangle to make a flying geese unit. Make 4 flying geese units.

Make 4

5. Arrange the half-square triangles and flying geese units as shown in the Double Star Block. Sew the blocks together in rows. Press the seams of each row to one side, alternating the direction with each row.

6. Sew the rows together to complete the block.

7. Repeat steps 1-6 to make a total of 9 Double Star Blocks in the blue colorway.

8. Repeat steps 1-6 to make 8 Double Star Blocks in each of the following colorways: pink, orange, purple, and yellow. Use the light, medium, and dark fabric from each colorway to create the blocks.

Assembling the Quilt Center

1. Lay out the 9 blue, 8 pink, 8 orange, 8 purple, and 8 yellow Double Star Blocks on a flat surface as shown in the *Sewing & Cutting Diagram*. Take care to place the blocks in the correct position to achieve the final quilt design.

2. Sew the blocks together into rows. Press the seams of each row to one side, alternating the direction with each row. Sew the rows together, adding the single block on the top row.

3. Press your quilt top with starch to prepare it for cutting. Referring to the *Sewing & Cutting Diagram*, use a pencil and ruler to mark the cutting lines and label the sections with arrows in the directions shown. Carefully cut the top into 3 sections on the pencil lines.

Note: Refer to page 9 if using the Cutting Guide and Arrow Guide Tape.

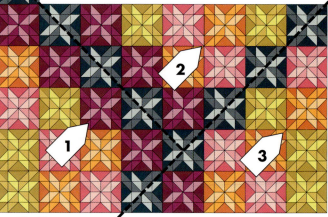

Sewing & Cutting Diagram

Cut First

4. Lay out the sections as shown in the *Reassemble Diagram* with the arrows pointing down. Sew the sections together and press. Trim the excess fabric in the corners with a square up ruler to complete the quilt center.

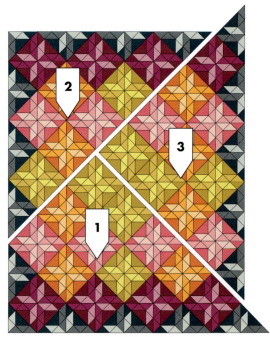

Reassemble Diagram

Making the Border Star Block

Pink Colorway
Make 11

Orange Colorway
Make 11

Purple Colorway
Make 14

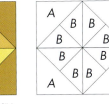

Yellow Colorway
Make 14

1. Lay out 4 dark pink A triangles, 4 medium pink B triangles, and 4 light pink B triangles as shown.

2. Sew a medium pink B triangle and a light B triangle together along the long edge to make a half-square triangle. Make 4 medium/light pink half-square triangles.

3. Sew the half-square triangles together in pairs, watching the direction of the triangles. Sew the pairs together to make the block center.

4. Sew a dark pink A triangle to opposite sides of the block center. Sew the remaining dark pink B triangles to the two remaining edges to complete the block. Make at total of 11 Border Star Blocks in the pink colorway.

5. Repeat steps 1-4 to make 11 orange colorway Border Star Blocks and 14 Border Star Blocks in colorways purple and yellow. Use the light, medium, and dark fabric from each colorway to create the blocks.

Making the Border Corner Block

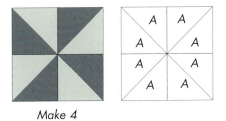

Make 4

1. Lay out 4 medium blue A triangles and 4 light blue A triangles, as shown.

2. Sew a medium blue A triangle and a light blue A triangle together along the long edge to make a half-square triangle. Make 4 medium/light blue half-square triangles.

3. Sew the half square triangles together in pairs, watching the direction of the triangles. Sew the pairs together to complete the block.

4. Repeat steps 1-3 to make a total of 4 blue Border Corner Blocks.

Adding the Inner Border

1. Sew the 1-1/2" dark blue border strips together to make one long strip.

2. Measure your quilt center from top to bottom and cut 2 side border strips to size. Sew the borders to the side edges of the quilt center. Press seams toward the border.

3. Measure your quilt center from side to side and cut 2 top/bottom border strips to size. Sew the borders to the top and bottom edges of the quilt center. Press seams toward the border.

Adding the Outer Border

1. Sew 14 yellow Border Star Blocks together end to end to make one long strip. Sew a dark yellow 3-1/2" x 6-1/2" rectangle to each end to make one yellow side border.

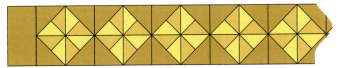

2. Repeat step 1 using 14 purple Border Star Blocks and dark purple 3-1/2" x 6-1/2" rectangles to make one purple side border.

3. Sew 11 pink Border Star Blocks together end to end to make one long strip. Sew a dark pink 3-1/2" x 6-1/2" rectangle to each end to make one pink top border.

4. Repeat step 3 using 11 orange Border Star Blocks and dark orange 3-1/2" x 6-1/2" rectangles to make one orange bottom border.

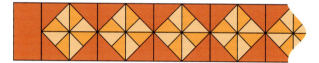

5. Measure your quilt center and cut the 4 border strip sections to size, measuring from the center out so the border design will be centered. Sew the yellow pieced side border to the left side of the quilt center and the purple pieced side border to the right side of the quilt center. Press seams toward the blue border.

6. Sew a blue Border Corner Block to each end of the orange and pink pieced borders. Sew the orange pieced bottom border to the bottom edge of the quilt center and the pink pieced top border to the top edge of the quilt center. Press seams toward the blue border.

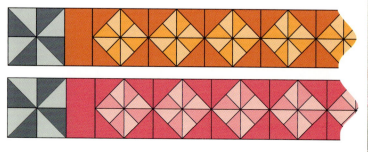

Finishing the Quilt

1. Sew the (3) 30" x 106" backing rectangles together along the long edges, using a 1/2" seam allowance. Press the seam allowance open.

2. Layer the backing, batting, and the quilt top. Baste the layers together and hand- or machine-quilt as desired.

3. Use diagonal seams to sew the 2-1/2"- wide dark blue binding strips together to make one long strip. Sew the binding to the edges of the quilt top.

4. Trim the extra batting and backing even with the edges of the quilt top. Turn the binding over the edge to the back and hand- or machine-sew in place.

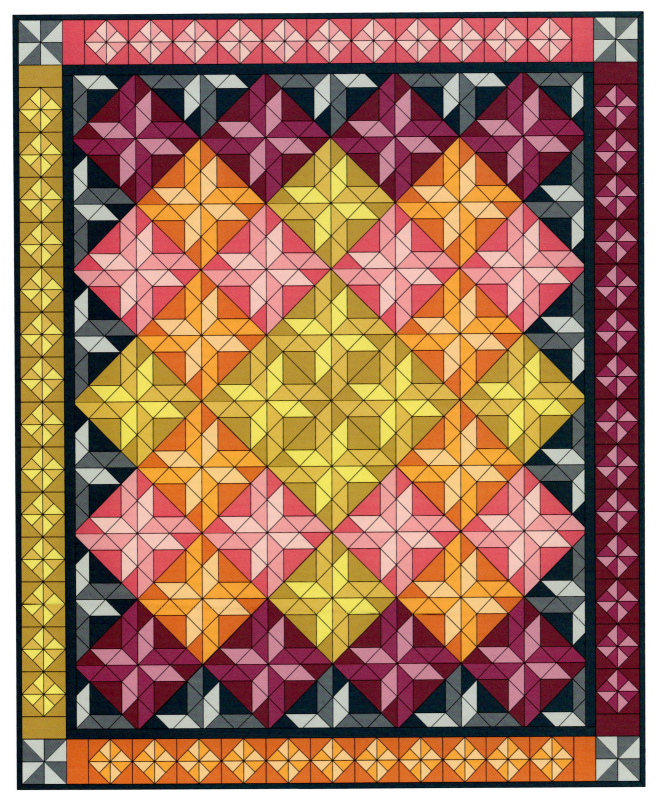

Super Nova

WATCHING THE WAVES

Pieced by Vicki Gersting; quilted by Bev's Machine Quilting

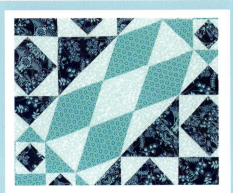

Finished Size:

80" x 97"

Block Size:

12" square

Materials

3-1/2 yards dark blue fabric for blocks and border

4 yards teal fabric for blocks and borders

3-1/4 yards white fabric for blocks and inner border

9 yards backing fabric

86" x 103" piece of batting

Refer to Square-agonals® Instructions and Sewing Tips on pages 7-10.

Storm at Sea Block

VIcki Block

Diamond Border Block

Square in Square Corner Block

Cutting Instructions

From dark blue fabric, cut:

(10) 4-7/8" x 40" strips.

From the strips, cut: (74) 4-7/8" squares. Cut the squares in half diagonally to make (148) D triangles for Storm at Sea Block and B triangles for Vicki Block.

(5) 4-1/2" x 40" strips.

From the strips, cut: (38) 4-1/2" G squares for Storm at Sea Block and A squares for Vicki Block.

(1) 3-3/8" x 40" strip.

From the strip, cut: (4) 3-3/8" B squares for Square in a Square Corner Border Block.

(13) 2-3/4" x 40" strips.

From the strips, cut: (88) 2-3/4" x 5-1/4" rectangles. Cut (44) rectangles in half diagonally from bottom left corner to top right corner to make (88) B triangles for Border Diamond Block.

Cut (44) rectangles in half diagonally from top left corner to bottom right corner to make (88) A triangles for Border Diamond Block.

(3) 2-1/2" x 40" strips.

From the strips, cut: (34) 2-1/2" E squares for Storm at Sea Block.

From teal fabric, cut:

(2) 12-1/2" x 40" strips.

From the strips, cut: (5) 12-1/2" squares.

(1) 4-1/2" x 40" strip.

From the strip, cut: (4) 4-1/2" A squares for Vicki Block.

(16) 4-1/8" x 40" strips.

From the strips, cut: (68) template I on page 93 for Storm at Sea Block and (44) template C on page 9 for Diamond Border Block.

(6) 2-7/8" x 40" strips.

    From the strips, cut: (76) 2-7/8" squares. Cut squares in half diagonally to make (152) C triangles for Storm at Sea Block and A triangles for Square in a Square Block.

(9) 2-1/2" x 40" strips for binding.

From white fabric, cut:

(6) 5-1/4" x 40" strips.

    From the strips, cut: (36) 5-1/4" squares. Cut the squares in quarters diagonally to make (144) H triangles for Storm at Sea Block and C triangles for Vicki Block.

    Cut (2) 4-7/8" squares. Cut squares in half diagonally to make (4) B triangles for Vicki Block.

(3) 3-1/4" x 40" strips.

    From the strips, cut: (34) 3-1/4" squares. Cut the squares in quarters diagonally to make (136) F triangles for Storm at Sea Block.

(20) 2-3/4" x 40" strips.

    From the strips, cut: (136) 2-3/4" x 5-1/4" rectangles. Cut (68) rectangles in half diagonally from bottom left corner to top right corner to make (136) A triangles for Storm at Sea Block.

    Cut (68) rectangles in half diagonally from top left corner to bottom right corner to make (136) B triangles for Storm at Sea Block.

(9) 1-1/2" x 40" strips for inner border.

From backing fabric, cut:

(3) 30" x 108" rectangles.

Making the Storm at Sea Block

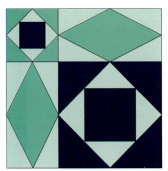

Make 34

1. Lay out 2 teal I diamonds, 4 teal C triangles, 4 white F triangles, 4 white A triangles, 4 white B triangles, 4 white H triangles, 4 dark blue D triangles, 1 dark blue E square and 1 dark blue G square, as shown. Mark all seam allowances for easy piecing.

2. Sew a white B triangle to the top left and bottom right sides of a teal I diamond, matching seam allowances. Sew a white A triangle to the top right and bottom left sides of the diamond, matching seam allowances. Make 2 diamond units.

3. Sew 2 white F triangles to opposite sides of a small dark blue E square. Sew 2 white F triangles to the remaining sides of the dark blue square to make 1 small square in a square unit.

4. Referring to step 3, sew (4) teal C triangles to the small square in a square center unit to complete the small square in a square unit.

5. Sew 2 white H triangles to opposite sides of a large dark blue G square. Sew 2 white H triangles to the remaining sides of the dark blue square to make 1 large square in a square center unit.

6. Referring to step 5, sew (4) dark blue D triangles to the large square in a square center unit square to make 1 large square in a square unit.

7. Sew the small square in a square unit and a diamond unit together for the top of the block.

8. Sew a diamond unit and the large square in a square unit together for the bottom of the block.

9. Sew the top and bottom of the block together to complete the Storm at Sea Block.

10. Repeat steps 1-9 to make a total of 34 Storm at Sea Blocks.

Making the Vicki Block

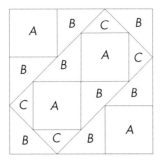

Make 2

1. Lay out 2 teal A squares, 2 dark blue A squares, 6 dark blue B triangles, 2 white B triangles, and 4 white C triangles, as shown. Mark all seam allowances for easy piecing.

2. Sew 2 dark blue B triangles to adjoining sides of the teal A square to make a corner triangle unit. Make 2 corner triangle units.

3. Sew 2 white C triangles to a adjoining sides of a dark blue A square. Sew a white B triangle to one of remaining sides. Make 2 square units. Sew the 2 square units together, as shown, to make the block center.

4. Sew a dark blue B triangle to each short end of the block center.

5. Sew the 2 triangle corner units to the long edges of the block center to complete the block.

6. Repeat steps 1-5 to make a total of 2 Vicki Blocks.

Assembling the Quilt Center

1. Lay out the 34 Storm at Sea Blocks, 2 Vicki Blocks, and 5 teal squares on a flat surface as shown in the *Sewing & Cutting Diagram*. Take care to place the blocks in the correct position to achieve the final quilt design.

2. Sew the blocks together into rows. Press the seams of each row to one side, alternating the direction with each row. Sew the rows together, adding the partial row on the bottom.

3. Press your quilt top with starch to prepare it for cutting. Referring to the *Sewing & Cutting Diagram*, use a pencil and ruler to mark the cutting lines and label the sections with arrows in the directions shown. Carefully cut the top into 3 sections on the pencil lines.

Note: Refer to page 9 if using the Cutting Guide and Arrow Guide Tape.

Sewing & Cutting Diagram   *Cut First*

4. Lay out the sections as shown in the *Reassemble Diagram* with the arrows pointing down. Sew the sections together and press. Trim the excess fabric in the corners with a square up ruler to complete the quilt center.

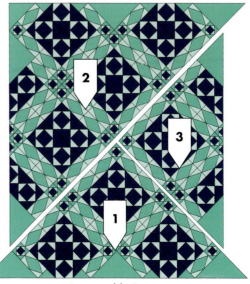

Reassemble Diagram

Making the Diamond Border Block

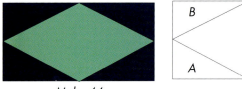 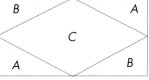

Make 44

Note: *This block finishes at 4" x 8".*

1. Lay out 1 teal C diamond, 2 dark blue A triangles, and 2 dark blue B triangles. Mark all seam allowances for easy piecing.

2. Sew a dark blue B triangle to the top left and bottom right sides of the teal C diamond, matching seam allowances. Sew a dark blue A triangle to the top right and bottom left sides of the diamond, matching seam allowances.

3. Repeat steps 1-2 to make a total of 44 Diamond Border Blocks.

Making the Square in a Square Corner Border Block

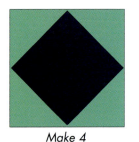 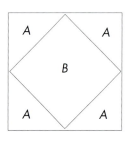

Make 4

1. Lay out 1 dark blue B square and 4 teal A triangles.

2. Sew 2 teal A triangles to opposite sides of the dark blue B square. Sew 2 teal A triangles to the remaining sides of the dark blue square to make one Square in a Square Corner Border Block.

3. Repeat steps 1-2 to make a total of 4 Square in a Square Border Corner Blocks.

Adding the Inner Border

1. Sew the 1-1/2" white border strips together to make one long strip.

2. Measure your quilt center from top to bottom and cut 2 side border strips to size. Sew the borders to the side edges of the quilt center. Press seams toward the border.

3. Measure your quilt center from side to side and cut 2 top/bottom border strips to size. Sew the borders to the top and bottom edges of the quilt center. Press seams toward the border.

Adding the Outer Border

1. Sew 12 Diamond Border Blocks together end to end to make one long strip for side border. Make 2 side borders.

2. Sew 10 Diamond Border Blocks together end to end to make one long strip for top/bottom border. Make 2 top/bottom borders.

3. Measure your quilt center and cut 4 border strip sections to size, measuring from the center out so the border design will be centered. The end diamonds will be cut through. Sew the borders to the left and right sides of the quilt center. Press seams toward the white border.

4. Sew a Square in a Square Border Corner Block to each end of the top/bottom borders. Sew the borders to the top and bottom edges of the quilt center. Press seams toward the white border.

Finishing the Quilt

1. Sew the (3) 30" x 108" backing rectangles together along the long edges, using a 1/2" seam allowance. Press the seam allowance open.

2. Layer the backing, batting, and the quilt top. Baste the layers together and hand- or machine-quilt as desired.

3. Use diagonal seams to sew the 2-1/2"- wide teal binding strips together to make one long strip. Sew the binding to the edges of the quilt top.

4. Trim the extra batting and backing even with the edges of the quilt top. Turn the binding over the edge to the back and hand- or machine-sew in place.

Storm at Sea Block
Templates

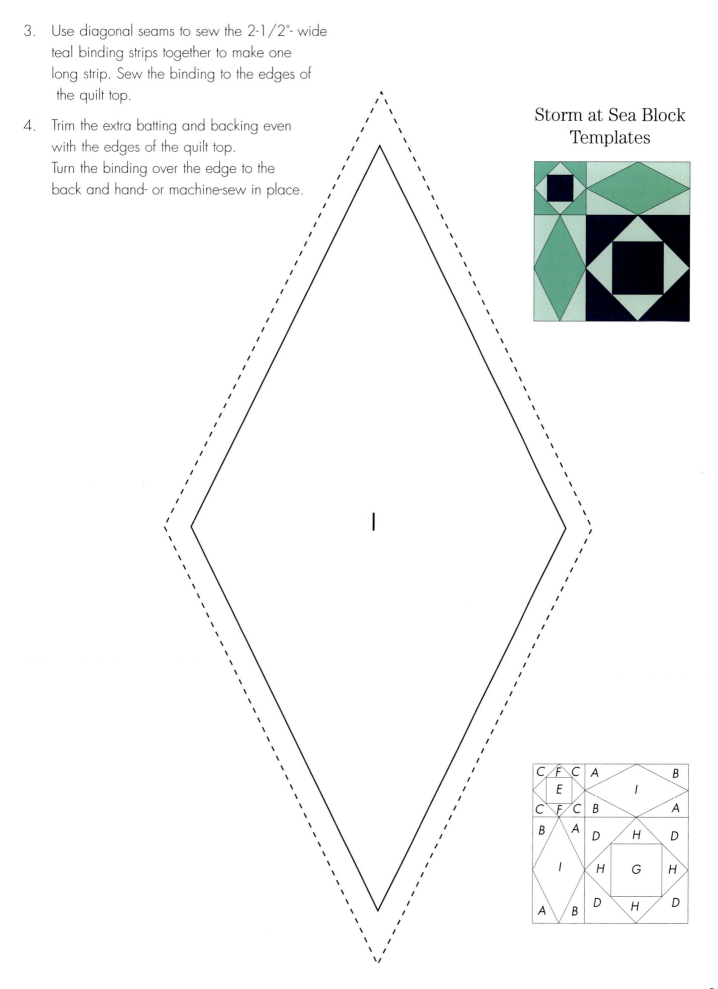

I

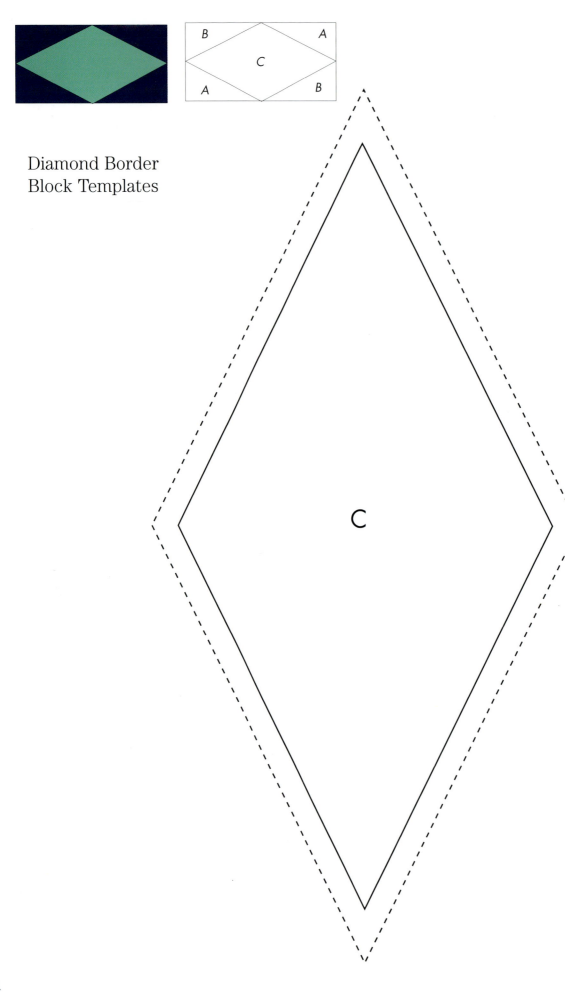

Diamond Border
Block Templates

C

Watching the Waves

Thanks and Acknowledgements

Special thanks to my husband Jack, my children Jonathan and Jessica, and the rest of my family.

The quilts in this book were made from the beautiful fabric collections of Art Gallery Fabrics.

Art Gallery Fabrics
www.artgalleryfabrics.com

AURIfil USA
www.aurifil.com

The Electric Quilt Company
www.electricquilt.com

The Warm™ Company
www.warmcompany.com

Finishing Touches Quilting Studio, LLC
www.finishingtouchesquiltingstudio.com

Bev's Machine Quilting
graysky@windstream.net

Blackstone Photography of WV
Wheeling, WV

Contact Sandi at: stitchedbuy@aol.com
Visit Sandi's website at: www.stitchedbuy.com

A very special thank you to the "Angels" of the BOM (Block Of the Month) Squad.
Your friendship, support, time and talent make my dreams come true.

Row 1: Stevie Robinson, Twila Toohill, Julia Plunkett, Vicki Gersting, and Linda Berry
Row 2: Rachel Kerekes, Judy Beveridge, and Krujetta Clark
Row 3: Beverly Gray, Linda Talasis, Susan Collins, me (Sandi Blackwell), and Pat Muth
Row 4: Ruth Ellen Fise, Ruth Ann Stevenson
Row 5: Donna Horstman, and Vicki Crawford
Not pictured: Leslie Allen, Michelle Parsons, Doris Turk, and Debbie Carpino